Shakespeare's Common Language

ARDEN SHAKESPEARE STUDIES IN LANGUAGE AND DIGITAL METHODOLOGIES

Series Editors: Jonathan Hope, Lynne Magnusson and Michael Witmore

Arden Shakespeare Studies in Language and Digital Methodologies seeks to identify, develop, and publish new work on Shakespeare and his contemporaries with a focus on language and/or digital methods.

Shakespearean Character: Language in Performance
Jelena Marelj
ISBN 978-1-3500-6138-5

FORTHCOMING
Reproducing English Renaissance Drama, 1711–2016
Brett Hirsch
ISBN 978-1-350-02186-0

Shakespeare's Common Language

Alysia Kolentsis

THE ARDEN SHAKESPEARE
LONDON • NEW YORK • OXFORD • NEW DELHI • SYDNEY

THE ARDEN SHAKESPEARE
Bloomsbury Publishing Plc
50 Bedford Square, London, WC1B 3DP, UK
1385 Broadway, New York, NY 10018, USA
29 Earlsfort Terrace, Dublin 2, Ireland

BLOOMSBURY, THE ARDEN SHAKESPEARE and the Arden Shakespeare logo are trademarks of Bloomsbury Publishing Plc

First published in Great Britain 2020
This paperback edition published in 2021

Copyright © Alysia Kolentsis, 2020

Alysia Kolentsis has asserted her right under the Copyright, Designs and Patents Act, 1988, to be identified as the author of this work.

For legal purposes the Acknowledgements on pp. vii–viii constitute an extension of this copyright page.

Series design by Louise Dugdale
Cover image: The description of Giles Mompesson
(© Folger Shakespeare Library)

Folger SHAKESPEARE LIBRARY

All rights reserved. No part of this publication may be reproduced or transmitted in any form or by any means, electronic or mechanical, including photocopying, recording, or any information storage or retrieval system, without prior permission in writing from the publishers.

Bloomsbury Publishing Plc does not have any control over, or responsibility for, any third-party websites referred to or in this book. All internet addresses given in this book were correct at the time of going to press. The author and publisher regret any inconvenience caused if addresses have changed or sites have ceased to exist, but can accept no responsibility for any such changes.

A catalogue record for this book is available from the British Library.

A catalog record for this book is available from the Library of Congress.

ISBN:	HB:	978-1-3500-0701-7
	PB:	978-1-3502-3597-7
	ePDF:	978-1-3500-0699-7
	eBook:	978-1-3500-0700-0

Series: Arden Shakespeare Studies in Language and Digital Methodologies

Typeset by Integra Software Services Pvt. Ltd.

To find out more about our authors and books visit www.bloomsbury.com and sign up for our newsletters.

CONTENTS

Note on the text vi
Acknowledgements vii

Introduction: Shakespeare's common language 1

1 *Coriolanus*: 'Mark you / His absolute "shall"?' 25

2 *Troilus and Cressida*: 'Do you think I will?' 63

3 *Richard II*: 'Here, cousin' 99

4 *As You Like It*: 'Much virtue in "if"' 133

Notes 162
References 175
Index 185

NOTE ON THE TEXT

All quotations from Shakespeare's plays and poems are taken from the Arden editions.

ACKNOWLEDGEMENTS

This book has been many years in the making, and those who have supported me as I've worked on it are legion. I could not have completed it without their advice, expertise and generosity.

My greatest debt is to Lynne Magnusson, supervisor, colleague and friend extraordinaire. I remain baffled that the universe arranged for two scholars independently interested in early modern English modal verbs to arrive at the University of Toronto at the same time, but I am grateful for this stroke of serendipity. I am also indebted to those who offered suggestions on the earliest version of this project: Alexandar Leggatt, Jeremy Lopez, Julian Patrick, Carol Percy, Paul Stevens and Paul Werstine. A special word of thanks goes to Kathy Acheson, my first mentor and champion, for introducing me to the wonders of early modern language and literature (and for providing the image for this book's cover). Thank you, as well, to Heather Dubrow, Diana Henderson and Patricia Parker; finding advocates in scholars whose work blazed the trail has been a gift. I always thought of Russ McDonald as my fairy godfather, for the doors he opened and the encouragement he offered when I most needed it. I hope he knew how much it meant to me.

I am particularly grateful to Ken Graham, the most generous colleague one could ask for. His comments on a draft of this book, along with his good cheer and his willingness to ponder topics from Shakespeare to baseball, have helped me immeasurably. Jonathan Hope's wonderful work has been a model for me from the beginning, and I am profoundly grateful for his support along the way, and for his insight and his suggestions on this project.

Lara Bateman, Mark Dudgeon, and the rest of the team at the Arden Shakespeare deserve much thanks for their work on the book. Funding from the Social Sciences and Humanities Research Council of Canada and a St Jerome's University Faculty Research Grant helped to support my research.

My years in academia have taught me that finding your people is the key to sustaining yourself. At the University of Toronto, my people included Dale Barleben, Amelia DeFalco, Erin Ellerbeck, Ann Park Lanpher, Katie Larson, Lindy Ledohowski, Chris Matusiak, Romi Mikulinsky, Jan Purnis, Virginia Strain and Alan Thompson. I'm grateful to each one of you; the bonds forged in graduate school are ironclad. I have had equal fortune in my colleagues at St Jerome's University and the University of Waterloo. For writing sessions and delicious baked treats, I thank Jolanta Komornicka. For chats about poetry and the marvels of form, I am grateful to Chad Wriglesworth. To Veronica Austen, Kelly Grindrod, Shana MacDonald and Sylvia Terzian: thank you for your wisdom, writing dates, moral support and much-needed levity. A special thank you, as well, to Nicole Irvine for her readiness to seek out fun and diversion.

To my parents Fran Kolentsis and Mike Kolentsis, my sister Neola Kolentsis, my aunt Margaret Davidson, and the Crosby-McEachern family, all of whom have helped me from the start: thank you. My grandmothers, Helen Kolentsis and Frances Cloney, whose sacrifices made possible the life I have today, would have been thrilled to know that I wrote a book. This is for them. Finally, to Mike Crosby and to our daughters, Lucia and Anna: you are the best gifts of all. Thank you for everything.

Introduction
Shakespeare's common language

In Shakespeare's England, 'common' was a rich and varied signifier. It could refer to the ordinary, mundane or frequent, but these meanings readily shaded into associations of the cheap and the vulgar. It could be a designation for 'the people' that referred broadly to the 'trew communes' that comprise the non-aristocratic class, or, less generously, to members of the social underclass who required containment (Howard and Strohm 549).[1] As an adjective, 'common' could also connote universality, something to which everyone is subject – as in Thersites' caustic reference to the 'common curse of mankind, folly and ignorance' (*TC* 2.3.27) – just as it could refer to a shared public space: 'the wide world's common place' (Sonnet 137.10). Its flexibility extends to its capacity to take up various parts of speech; in addition to its function as a capacious adjective, it worked as a noun: 'Your sauciness will jest upon my love / And make a common of my serious hours' (*CE* 2.2.29). Like all words, it is inherently polysemous, yet as its functional and semantic range suggests, 'common' in sixteenth-century England was pointedly double-edged. Depending on the stance and motivation of the speaker, it could be a slur or an avowal, a claim for solidarity or a marker of distance. For early modern

English writers such as Shakespeare, 'common' offered ample opportunity for easy punning. When Gertrude points to the universal cycle of life and death to suggest that Hamlet's grief is unnatural – 'Thou knowest 'tis common all that lives must die,' Hamlet rebukes her by throwing the word back with its meaning emphatically shifted: 'Ay, madam, it is common' (*Ham* 1.2.72, 74). More amusingly, in *Love's Labour's Lost*, Maria insists 'My lips are no common sir, though several they be' (2.1.209).

Just as the word itself accented the potential both to unite and to divide, the idea of a 'common language' symbolized both promise and threat to citizens of sixteenth-century England. Rhetoricians and religious reformers alike used the ideal of a 'common tongue' as a launching point for arguments of universality and accessibility. To Protestant reformers, the availability of scripture in a 'common tongue' was an inviolable cornerstone of the movement. Debates about the translation of scripture flourished in sixteenth-century England. Miles Coverdale, defending his path-breaking English Bible, argued that (informally, at least) there was widespread agreement on the basic principle 'that the common praier of the Church should be had in the common tongue' (1564). In 1578, the Protestant Philip Caesar condemned Catholic dissenters – characterizing them as 'ungrateful' and 'wicked against God' – while at the same time tracing a link between the common tongue and the belief that all human beings are capable of virtue:

> Whereby it is apparent, how iniurious they are to their brethren, how vngratefull to their countrie, how wicked against God, whiche mislike, speake, inueigh against the bringing either of the worde of God, or the workes of good men agreable to his wil, into a *common tongue*. As though that either God could be too muche honored, or godlinesse of too many practised: as though vertue could bee too *common*, or for some kinde of men to be vertuous were not commendable. (emphasis added)

In this passage, Caesar shrewdly aligns the common tongue with common humanity. He challenges the pejorative equation of the 'common' with the unsavoury, insisting that traits such as the potential for virtue and godliness are universal; therefore, in order to realize this common potential, the 'worde of God' must be made available in the common tongue. Arguments put forward by reformers such as Coverdale, Caesar and Tyndale – who wrote, 'Euen so it is not inough to haue translated, though it were ye whole Scripture into the vulgare & common toung' – tended to conflate 'common' and 'vulgar' language. In claims for accessible scripture, the 'common tongue' is necessarily English. Yet some counter arguments differentiated between 'common' and 'vulgar' in order to make a case for the purity of the original language of the Bible:

> Concerning that you read Gods word to the people at you Church seruice tyme in the vulgar tungs, it is no perfection at all on your syde. For yee lack thereby the vse of the better tungs, as of the Greek and Latin: which were sanctified on Christes crosse as for all other holy vses, so most specially for to serue God withall at the tyme of Sacrifice, wherein he requireth the very best in euery kind to be offered vnto him, as to our dreadful Lord, and louing father. And who douteth, but that a lerned, a holy, and a common tung, is more honorable, then a barbarouse, a prophane, and a priuate tung? In so much, that in respect of the whole body of the Catholike Church (wherewith we specially communicate in our seruice and praiers) the vulgare tungs are much more to be accompted strange or vnknowen (which strange tungs onely S. Paule doth least regard) then the common tungs, which were alone deliuered to the very first Christian Churche, by the Apostles themselues, in the East and West. (Sander, *The rocke of the Churche*)

Here, Sander inverts arguments about accessibility and universality. In his assessment, 'common' is a known quantity, a standard whose authority is emphasized when set in opposition to the strange and variable 'private' and 'vulgar' tongues. Drawing on traditional assumptions about the linguistic superiority of Latin and Greek, Sander aligns these apparently elevated tongues with the 'common'. According to his argument, the language that was common to the Apostles, and which was used as the original language of the Bible, is dishonorably lost among diverse and distorting vernaculars.

Sixteenth-century debates about 'common language' also flourished in humanist circles. Language reformers sought for English to realize its potential as a sophisticated and authoritative language that was capable of holding its own among the ascendant vernacular tongues of places such as Italy and Spain.[2] Central to these shifting notions about the status of English were debates about the relative merits of Latin and English. By mid-century, general perceptions about the relationship between classical and vernacular language were changing, yet tension remained. Vestiges of older beliefs – that systematized grammar rules were exclusive to Latin and that English was a vulgar and disordered tongue – coexisted with burgeoning ideas about the capacity of English to have its own set of rules, different from but equal to those of Latin (Görlach, 'Regional and Social Variation' 482). Language purists also discouraged the practice of importing new words from Latin and other Latinate languages and instead advocated for speakers to coin new words from existing Saxon forms to augment the English lexicon. The scholar Sir John Cheke, a vocal proponent of native vocabulary-building, took on the improbable project of translating the New Testament using only English terms.[3] Other reformers focused on the English grammar school curriculum's dependence on Latin, and pedagogical treatises lamenting the lack of English in the classroom began to proliferate. Richard Mulcaster, headmaster at the distinguished Merchant Taylors' and St Paul's schools, argued for the attenuation of Latin instruction so that English schoolboys could become better acquainted with the beauty of their native tongue. Mulcaster famously derided the 'bondage' that saw English speakers become servants to Latin, while neglecting the 'treasur in our own tung': 'I loue *Rome*, but *London* better, I fauor *Italie*, but England more, I honor the Latine, but I worship the *English*' (254).

As scholars and rhetoricians wrestled with questions about the relative status of vernacular and classical language, they regularly invoked the notion of the 'common' to position vernacular rhetorics as tools for fostering national community. In the *Arte or Crafte of Rhetoryke* (1532) Leonard Cox justifies his use of English by drawing on a positive association of 'common'; more common, he claims, means more accessible and therefore superior. He notes that his work is:

> Partely translated out a werke of Rhetorique wryten in the Latin tongue: and partely compiled of myne owne: and so made a little treatyse in maner of an Introductyon into this aforesaid Science: and that in our Englyshe tongue. Remembrynge that euery good thing (after the sayengs of the Philosopher) the more comon it is: the more better it is.

As Jenny C. Mann observes, Cox's argument here turns on the multivalent associations of the word 'common'. In one sense, it is the 'common' citizen of England, lacking social status and the accompanying advantages of Latin education, who has much to gain from Cox's *Rhetoryke*. Yet 'common' also suggests something that belongs and relates to all: 'the shared possession constitutes a coherent group where none existed before. In this case the common possession is the English language ... Cox concludes that anyone who wishes to be "regarded" as part of this national community will desire to read his translated text' (39). Many rhetorical manuals in the years following Cox's followed his lead in invoking the language of common profit. The burgeoning field of English rhetoric was thus underscored by a commitment to 'unit[ing] country folk with Elizabethan courtiers in a shared cause against the tyranny of pedantic clerks who would restrict access to the arts of discourse' (Mann 41).[4]

The impassioned linguistic debates of this era could not help but filter into public consciousness. Citizens of sixteenth-century England saw the vernacular making gradual incursions against the dominant force of Latin, and at the same time, they became accustomed to the distinct features of and tensions between classical and native language:

> What Cheke and other mid-sixteenth-century purists ... achieve[d] by resisting the Latinate invasion and defending the dignity of native 'Saxon' English was to develop a general awareness of the etymological origin of words and an appreciation that the Saxon and Latinate elements in the word-stock had different and complementary expressive properties. (Adamson, 'Literary Language' 573)

Given the context of awareness to the nuances and origins of words, writers such as Shakespeare could play on the tension between Latin and English to creative ends in their work. In addition to his appreciation of the expressive possibilities of the vernacular, Shakespeare consistently draws attention to foundational Saxon words that form the cornerstone of everyday speech.

In highlighting 'common' in this book, my goal is to underscore the constellation of associations for the word 'common' in early modern English: the sense of a shared set of linguistic resources on which all speakers depend; the notion of the language belonging to all of its users, regardless of social status; the pejorative associations of uncouth and barbaric speech, opposed to the polished and ornate; the elements of language that are so familiar that they are rendered virtually transparent. A related concern of this book is thinking about how circulating notions of the 'common' in Shakespeare's England might be applied to Shakespeare's commitment, realized in a variety of ways, to common forms of language. Language is fundamentally and definitively common; necessarily shared, it is subject to all of the tensions that accompany a collective asset. Aspects of my analysis in this book derive from the conflicts that emerge among speakers attempting to negotiate their claims on shared language, and the ways that they must reckon with its necessary dependence on others. I am also interested in another understanding of 'common' language: the quotidian words that comprise the easily overlooked background noise of dialogue. In this book, I suggest that Shakespeare's common language, and specifically the seemingly neutral words that make up the nuts-and-bolts elements of dialogue, are the animating engines of Shakespeare's writing. Functional terms and other common words tend to be overlooked as sources of literary meaning, but they pack a formidable expressive punch. Throughout his plays and poems, Shakespeare draws our attention to the common words of his language, jolting them out of their familiar contexts to encourage us to see them with new eyes. My aim in this book is to do the same, so that we might appreciate the small words of Shakespeare's language in new ways.

***

FALSTAFF
    No, my good lord; banish Peto,
    banish Bardolph, banish Poins – but for sweet Jack
    Falstaff, kind Jack Falstaff, true Jack Falstaff,
    valiant Jack Falstaff, and therefore more valiant,
    being, as he is old Jack Falstaff, banish not him
    thy Harry's company, banish not him thy Harry's
    company, banish plump Jack, and banish all the world.

PRINCE HENRY
    I do, I will.

(*1H4* 2.4.468–75)

In this scene from *King Henry IV, Part 1*, Falstaff and Prince Henry (or Hal, as his friends at the tavern call him) playact an imagined future in which Hal becomes king and must renounce the loutish company he keeps. Falstaff's teasing plea for clemency is abruptly deflated by Hal's terse response. Much is accomplished in the space of four syllables.

I do, I will: the simple, repeated and quintessentially common formula of pronoun and verb captures an expansive narrative about duty, desire and necessary outcomes. Hal's promise both reflects his calculated strategy and foreshadows the necessity of his relinquishment of all vestiges of his former life, Falstaff included, when he becomes king. Striking monosyllables such as these recur in Shakespeare's poems and plays. Consider Lear's 'O, you are men of stones!' (*KL* 5.3.255) or Iago's 'I am not what I am' (*Oth* 1.1.71). And while Shakespeare, in the popular imagination, tends to be held up as a prolific inventor of memorable words – many of which are merely attributed to and not coined by Shakespeare – it is his dexterous use of ordinary words and phrases such as 'I do, I will' that is his most arresting linguistic skill.

The proliferation of searchable online databases in recent years has been a boon for scholars with an interest in Shakespeare's language. Digital concordances offer a delightful miscellany of lexical details, such as the number of instances of a particular word in Shakespeare's canon, and, more generally, the most frequently used words in the plays. Not surprisingly, the most common words are primarily comprised of the pronouns, prepositions and conjunctions that are the foundations of English syntax: *the, and, is, with, I, you* and the like. Readers and auditors are accustomed to registering these words in a different way than they do content words, such as the inventive nouns for which Shakespeare is so famous. This selective linguistic reception makes an intuitive sort of sense; efficient comprehension depends upon an unconscious ranking system for the words that make up a sentence or an utterance. We don't grant equal weight to the functional terms that scaffold all utterances as we do to the words that make such utterances unique.[5] In most cases, it makes good sense to relegate the common words to the background din of comprehension. When Hamlet exclaims, 'O, what a rogue and peasant slave am I!' (*Ham* 2.2.485), it is the powerful adjectives and nouns to which we are drawn (why a 'rogue' and 'peasant'? 'slave' to whom or what?) rather than to the rote 'a,' 'and' and 'am' (the resounding line ending 'I', though, echoes meaningfully, and offers a good illustration of the larger argument of this project: even among flashy content words, the functional ones can resonate). So quotidian that they fade into the background, common words are too easily deemed neutral or insignificant. Yet these 'small words', as Sylvia Adamson has fittingly labelled them ('Understanding Shakespeare's Grammar' 210), perform the understated heavy lifting of linguistic expression. Heavily context dependent, small words yield much information about speakers and the nature of their speech. In addition to their grammatical duties, they enact important expressions of identity, stance and opinion. In this book, I want to emphasize the ways that some of the most foundational questions that literary critics ask of dramatic works (and of literary texts more broadly) rely on the expressive potential of small words: How is meaning made in this work? How are impressions of character created and reinforced? How is dramatic action embedded and realized in dialogue? Very often, the foundation for this type of analysis may be found in expressions of person (pronouns and forms of self-reference such as *I* and *we*), modal verbs of volition and intention like *will* and *shall*, contextualizing words such as *now, here* and *this*, and indicators of conditions or wished-for alternative outcomes like *if*.

The book helps to illuminate how the common words used by Shakespeare's speakers encode significant clues about interaction and interpersonal relationships. Indeed, the minute details of linguistic encounters hold important information about speakers' perceptions of themselves, their interlocutors and their environment. Attention to such details, and to charged moments of linguistic encounter in which speakers must negotiate their modes of self-positioning, highlights the troubled processes of self-representation and changing self-perception, and throws into relief moments of interaction which are pivotal to dramatic texts.

In addition to highlighting the expressive and interpersonal force of common words, *Shakespeare's Common Language* shines a light on approaches to language that may fruitfully be put to use in the study of Shakespeare's language. Each chapter of the book is structured around a language-based approach, one or two representative common words, and one play. The methodologies of each chapter range from specialized (discourse analysis, pragmatics and deixis) to broad (language change and grammar). Broadly derived from the field of linguistics, these approaches isolate the details of linguistic exchange, and particularly elements of dialogue and other explicitly socially oriented forms of language. Linguistics and its sister fields have produced a great deal of compelling work over the past several decades, much of it with a direct bearing on dialogue. While a few key studies have brought this work to bear on Shakespeare in illuminating ways, there remains an opportunity for further productive research. As I will discuss, there tends to be among literary scholars an understandable resistance to borrowing categories from non-literary disciplines and importing them wholesale onto works of literature. The spectre of anachronism heightens these concerns; it's one matter to apply language theories developed out of patterns in present-day English to contemporary dramatic works, and quite another to do the same to 400-year-old plays. The chapters that follow maintain an awareness of the tensions between early modern and contemporary forms of the language, as well as the sometimes disparate demands of 'actual' and literary speech. The approaches that are explored and developed in these chapters represent not simply a blanket application of contemporary theory onto Shakespeare's language, but rather a contextualized and historicized understanding of his linguistic choices and usage. My goal in articulating these approaches is the creation of an interdisciplinary base that combines linguistic theory with literary analysis, one that is alert to historical contexts and changes. What can recent innovative developments in contemporary linguistics and language theory bring to bear on Shakespeare's language? How might rhetorical and linguistic features that have always been of interest to literary scholars be complemented and augmented by other approaches to language? This book suggests that these approaches can offer rich information for critics of literature and can yield information that sharpens our understanding of how meaning is made in literary works.

As I will discuss further, the language under scrutiny in *Shakespeare's Common Language* is significant because it is intended for performance and is therefore subject to influences of theatre-specific time, space and audience. Just as important to this study, though, is the fact that the language, and particularly the grammar, available to Shakespeare is demonstrably different than that of contemporary English speakers. In early modern England, the very term 'grammar' had a wider and less pejorative semantic base: 'Grammar was not, as now, a term reserved for basic pedagogy or a science within semantics, although it was both of these as well. It was the *ars* before and within every other *ars* … Grammar as a word therefore covered the full range of the linguistic and the literary, the semantic and the semiotic' (Cummings, *Literary Culture* 21). Moreover, the structure of the language itself was undergoing unusually rapid transformation during the period concurrent with Shakespeare's lifetime, a particularly vibrant moment in the history of English. Shakespeare's English was a language in transition: it was engaged in the process of written standardization and its global status was on the rise (Hope, 'Shakespeare's "Natiue English"' 243). In addition, it was transforming into what is recognized as 'modern' English, gradually shedding many of its earlier syntactic and lexical forms. These factors converged to produce a fruitful and varied pool of linguistic resources, ideal fodder for writers, and particularly for playwrights, whose craft depended on vibrant and modish dialogue. The common words *shall* and *will*, discussed in Chapters 1 and 2, exemplify an aspect of this English-in-flux which merits particularly close attention. The modal verbs represent a locus of linguistic change and act as exemplars for the transitional nature of English in the early modern period. Knowledge of the grammatical choices available to Shakespeare, and an analysis of the various nuanced ways he exploits them, opens new windows of interpretation into perennial questions of the identity, consciousness and motivation of his characters. By examining easily overlooked lexical and grammatical features – lynchpins of conversations such as assertions of self and other in personal pronouns, verbal assertions of desire and obligation in *will* and *shall*, indications of physical and emotional distance in *this* and *that*, and the conditions and possibilities indicated by *if* – this study participates in what Brian Cummings aptly calls an 'archaeology of grammar': a close examination of the methods and patterns of literary language, 'an excavation of the hidden processes and recesses of discourse' (*Literary Culture* 12).

During the heyday of historicist approaches, linguistic studies of Shakespeare generally fell out of favour. In the mid-1990s, Patricia Parker in *Shakespeare from the Margins* reflected that studies of the context, history and artistry of Shakespeare's language were suffering from a period of neglect and curious critical ennui. Attention to Shakespeare's language, Parker argued, was victim to a sense of 'inconsequentiality ... not only by the influence of neoclassicism but by continuing critical assumptions about the transparency (or unimportance) of the language of the plays' (13). In the two decades following Parker's assertion, the picture has begun to change. There has been a resurgence of interest in formal, stylistic and linguistic approaches to Shakespeare and studies have appeared that consider Shakespeare's style, his linguistic innovation, and taxonomies of his grammar, among other topics. However, there have been relatively few attempts in Shakespeare studies to integrate adequately the fields of language theory and literary criticism. A gap remains, and fruitful developments in linguistics and pragmatics have only occasionally been brought to bear on Shakespeare's language in a comprehensive way. This book is part of a small movement that attempts to repair the gap by demonstrating how recent developments in language criticism can uncover fruitful new approaches to Shakespeare's work, while also historicizing Shakespeare's language to take into account the critical effects (and creative potential) of language change and linguistic variation. The methodologies tested out in the chapters that follow grow out of the conviction that recent developments in language criticism – categories borrowed from the studies of grammar, linguistics, pragmatics and discourse analysis – have much to offer those of us with an interest in Shakespeare's language. By treating a selection of plays from various time periods and genres, the book explores a diverse sample of Shakespeare's dramatic language.

The field of linguistics has a long, and sometimes fraught, history within literary studies. At the beginning of the twentieth century, Ferdinand de Saussure's landmark *Course in General Linguistics* (1913) loosened the scientific tether on the field of linguistics, suggesting that linguistic forms and methods could have widespread applications in any communicative system – not only written and spoken language – and so became the foundation for the discipline-spanning study of semiotics. This multidisciplinary tendency was also evident in the fusion of the work of the linguist Roman Jakobson and the anthropologist Claude Lévi-Strauss; a meeting between the two figureheads left Lévi-Strauss convinced that 'phonology (the study of linguistic sounds) could provide a methodological basis for all the human sciences, and thus laid the path towards the French structuralism of the 1950s and 1960s, in which linguistics inspired a range of disciplines' (Fabb 3). While the binary-dismantling queries of critics like Barthes and Derrida are by now in our collective rearview mirror, a literary study that is rooted in linguistic approaches cannot help but be coloured by the influence of the structuralists and the critics who followed them. Structuralism casts a long shadow; distinctions such as Saussure's ideas of *langue* and *parole*, and Chomsky's contiguous notions of *competence* and *performance* inform present-day understandings of the special characteristics of speech in general and dramatic language in particular. Similarly, Jakobson's pioneering understanding of language production as a result of the processes of selection and combination – and his wider assertions about the self-consciousness of language production, that in using language speakers draw attention to its formal structure – placed an emphasis not only on lexical meaning but also on the significance of the choices made by speakers.

More central than structuralism to the methodologies of this book is the criticism that has come out of the wake of formalist approaches, and particularly those that integrate the tools of structural analysis with the contextualizing tendencies of movements such as new historicism. *Shakespeare's Common Language* joins a modest number of studies that respond to the polarization in literary studies between formal textual approaches and frameworks rooted in historical or cultural approaches. Lynne Magnusson has identified the distance between 'the conceptual orientation to language as a social phenomenon and the analytical tools'; she argues that, in contemporary literary analysis, 'the demonstration of how deconstructive readings manifest social determination or constraint in language use is missing' (*Shakespeare and Social Dialogue* 7). Like the work of Magnusson, Sylvia Adamson, Jonathan Hope, Hugh Craig and others, the methods of this book attempt to draw the poles closer, using the tools of linguistic methodology and discourse analysis to produce readings that are anchored in historical and cultural contexts, and which acknowledge the foundational importance of social interaction and exchange.[6]

Although some division between formalist and post-structuralist approaches is still evident on the landscape of literary studies, the strict formalism of mid-century linguistic theory has softened considerably. Part of the legacy left to contemporary literary scholars by the structuralists and their successors is the ever-broadening application of linguistic methods. The abstract linguistic theory of Saussure – with its Platonic trees and 'sound-images' – has given way to theories that are more grounded in actual, experiential contexts of communication. The early formalist assumption that linguistic form is distinct from the world of objective reality, governed by a unified system of symbols in which meanings are arbitrary and unhinged from their points of reference, has transformed into a recognition of contextual significance. In particular, the emphasis in linguistic studies over the past fifty years has shifted from sentences considered in isolation to language in use. One prominent example is an influential 1972 article by the linguist Dell Hymes that challenged Noam Chomsky's well-known formulation of linguistic competence. In a Chomskyan sense, competence is defined as the linguistic knowledge of an ideal language user, and it follows that a user with competence has an innate recognition of the grammaticality of a language. Hymes asserted that, in fact, there is more to competence than merely the stringing together of a grammatically sound sentence; another fundamental component to communication is, for example, appropriateness, the judgement of whether such a sentence is effective in or suited to the given context. According to Hymes, linguistics ought to concern itself with communicative competence, the speaker's ability to produce appropriate utterances, not grammatical sentences (282). Other linguists, taking up Hymes' exhortation, began to work under the assumption that *utterances*, not sentences, should be the central concern of linguistics: 'The sentence is an abstract entity in linguistics, defined in relation to particular grammars, and not in absolute terms. Utterances bring back into the reckoning the contextual factors which are abstracted away by grammatical sentences. Utterances are relevant to areas of language in use; sentences to grammar' (Herman, *Dramatic Discourse* 13).

The scholarship of the past several decades has progressively recognized and explored the interactive nature of linguistic practice: the act of communication that undergirds linguistic exchange is necessarily social, and is thus bound up in a system of relational forces and counter-forces. This means that potential objects of study – including literary works – are part of this system of social exchange, and a linguistic approach must acknowledge that meaning is derived relationally. Part of the 'external' network of relations informing my approach in this book is historical context; as I will argue, the peculiar characteristics of Shakespeare's grammar – and more specifically, the range of grammatical choices open to speakers in Shakespeare's age due to the transitional quality of a rapidly changing English language – directly affect the meanings that we may attach to his lexical and grammatical choices. Equally significant to meaning-making is the 'internal' network of language, in which, as the formative work of Mikhail Bakhtin and others has shown, utterances are dialogically constructed, always contingent and interdependent. Language is a social phenomenon, a continuous generative process that unfolds in verbal interaction between speakers. Relationships are created, tested and reinforced in each linguistic encounter, even those that seem neutral or innocuous: 'By looking at the grammatical choices speakers make, the role they play in discourse, we have a way of uncovering and studying the social creation and maintenance of hierarchic, socio-cultural roles' (Eggins 187). *Shakespeare's Common Language* focuses on interactive linguistic encounters and utterances that are situated in specific contexts. The wide-scale context is the literary discourse of Shakespeare's works. As I discuss below, dramatic dialogue falls into a specialized category due to its multiple functions: public, private and performative. The more immediate context is the dialogic exchanges within the dramatic discourse, which expose meaningful factors such as relative social status and powerful motivators such as fear and desire.

Because some of the language-based approaches of this book were derived from and designed for the study of 'real-world' dialogue, readers may wonder about the pitfalls of importing methodologies from one specialized field to another. There are several threads to tease out here. First, approaches to language such as discourse analysis were developed by linguists, sociologists and anthropologists; as a result, their tools and methods are designed to highlight elements of language that are of interest to fields other than literary studies, and which are in many cases far removed from the concerns of literary critics. Notions of discursively inscribed power, politeness and negotiation are complicated and muddied by the aesthetic demands of literary language. Moreover, Shakespeare's language is, of course, not the 'discourse' studied by discourse analysts, but rather a literary representation of dialogue, reflective of a specialized social, historical and linguistic context and designed to be spoken under the conditions of theatrical performance. How might linguistic approaches devised by social scientists to assess patterns of actual dialogue in a twentieth-century context be brought to bear on the works of an early modern playwright without grave simplification or distortion? To begin to answer this question, we must interrogate the assumption of the absolute division between actual and fictionalized dialogue. While there are clear differences between the two types, it is not the case that they are governed by distinct rules and mandates. Literary dialogue does not represent a radical break with what we see in actual, spontaneous dialogue. The difference appears to be one of degree: if we think of 'real' dialogue as a mélange of repetitions, hedges and hesitations, then its fictionalized counterpart is like a concentrated version of that mixture: 'Literary dialogue constitutes a competence model for interaction. It is not equivalent to the dialogue spontaneously produced in interaction.' In contrast, it contains 'occasional rather than pervasive repetition, hesitations, slips, false starts, and so on'. It thus 'distills the wheat of conversation from the chaff of hesitations, fillers, hedges, and repetitions' (Tannen 261). As linguist Deborah Tannen argues, the rules governing dialogue in fictional discourse are more pronounced, and this emphasis on the contours and meaning-making properties of dialogue allows for literary dialogue to act as a competence model. The linguist and literary scholar Vimala Herman, in a study focused specifically on dramatic dialogue, makes a similar claim. In creating dialogue, dramatists highlight 'underlying speech conventions, principles and "rules" of use … [the] conventions of use which underlie spontaneous communication in everyday life are precisely those which are exploited and manipulated by dramatists in their constructions of speech types and forms in plays' (*Dramatic Discourse* 6). Here, Herman suggests that the rules governing actual dialogue are the very things that dramatists are attuned to and tend to exploit in their work; as a result, dramatic dialogue tends to distill and highlight key components of actual dialogue. Rather than characterize the relationship between 'real' and dramatic discourse as one of separation, it is more viable to see them as a continuum, and there is good reason to treat methodologies such as discourse analysis as approaches that can shed light on both literary and actual dialogue.

As written language emulating speech, with the intention of performance, dramatic dialogue employs strategies and acquires meanings that are particular to the context of the stage. In his discussion of theatrical semiosis, Keir Elam explains the peculiar transformational power ascribed to theatre, citing the Russian formalist Petr Bogatyrev's thesis 'that the stage radically transforms all objects and bodies defined within it, bestowing upon them an overriding signifying power which they lack – or which at least is less evident – in their normal social functions' (7). In addition to the objects and bodies of which the stage makes signs, we can include the category of language, for the signifying power of words on stage is inextricable from their theatrical context. Dramatic language urges us to succumb to its mimetic power, and to erase its boundaries of artifice. The common words of Shakespeare under consideration in this book have the specialized characteristic, first, of being written representations of speech, so that they are undergirded by specific assumptions: they are to be understood as being spoken aloud, shared with an interlocutor, and subject to the off-the-cuff production characteristic of real dialogue. Indeed, despite the quality of 'literariness' ascribed to dramatic dialogue, it shares a foundation with non-literary discourse which is in some ways more salient than its affinities to other literary modes. The conventions and characteristics of conversation are relevant to dramatic language because both exist in a context of social interaction; both are 'speech exchange systems, which sets them apart from poetic genres like the ode or the lyric, or narrator language in the novel' (Herman, 'Deixis and Space' 3). It is this common base – the rules and nuances of interactive and 'realistic' speech behaviour – that dramatic productions expose and exploit. While dramatic speech is clearly distinct from 'actual' speech, the conventions and strategies of the dialogue spoken on stage tend to be in line with other non-literary types of dialogue.

Additionally, the language of drama, like spoken language generally, is *situated*; it is embedded in a unique spatio-temporal context and involves certain participants who are themselves anchored in a predetermined space. The idiosyncrasies of dramatic language throw the conventions and conduct of relationships between participants into relief: 'Stage dialogue, by its very nature, exposes acts of verbal manipulation and violence to a kind of scrutiny not normally possible in real life and in doing so sets up implicit norms of "correct" interpersonal discourse' (Dodd, 'Destined Livery?' 157). Moreover, these participants are, first and foremost, *speakers* – their dialogue is the primary means by which we gain access, and their words comprise the foundation of our judgements. It is interesting that the root of the word 'person' – *persona*, a mask through which sound travels – derives from the terminology of the stage and has at its core the notion of communication.[7] A character – a 'person' – is defined by and is a product of the speech that they produce.

It should be emphasised that there are important ways in which the language spoken by characters onstage remains distinct from the language of social interaction. The uniqueness of dramatic speech lies in the fact that, despite its ostensible distance from other literary genres and its frequent appearance of an anti-literary tilt, it remains as subject to the frame of literary analysis as lyric poetry or narrative fiction. The language of a dramatic production, unlike that of a conversation, has the additional feature of being intended for the stage – words in this arena are not only representations of speech, but also of performance. The conditions of the stage infuse the words of a dramatic text, so that the awareness of their performative potential conditions all possible associations and meanings. Another important consequence of the context of performance is that dramatic speakers do not simply address other performers; their words are also intended for the audience offstage. The effect of this doubly intended speech disrupts typical reception patterns, for in this case there are additional interlocutors. It is not simply the ostensible addressees on stage to whom the words matter, but also the shadow addressees in the audience, who assume the role of mere eavesdroppers even as they are, of course, just as implicated in the exchange as the performers that they are observing. We must also be mindful of distinctions between characters onstage and the more broadly understood category of speakers, and accordingly tread with caution in attributing speech effects such as volition and agency to Shakespeare's dramatic characters. Yet 'character is a palpable emotional reality on stage' (Maguire 154), and audiences and readers must be able to react to characters as something resembling speaking persons with discernable agency and decision-making capacity. While it is problematic to equate 'character' with subjectivity and intentionality, these features are products character 'effects': 'critics who reject the post-romantic view of a character as an autonomous agent endowed with a unique inner essence, tend to treat a character's "subjectivity" not as a location or content or property but as an effect – typically (though not uniquely) an effect of friction between discourses' (Dodd, 'Destined Livery?' 150). Indeed, it is precisely this friction – the interplay of dialogue among characters, the intersubjective space between speakers onstage – that is illuminated by the common words that are central to this book.

* * *

Each chapter that follows focuses on one play, reviews a particular approach derived from the field of linguistics or language theory, and explores its uses in attending to and understanding key 'common' words that are brought to light using that approach. It's critical to note from the outset the artificial nature of this arrangement. In pairing particular plays with specific methodologies, I do not mean to suggest that there is an essential or necessary link between the two. The methods of analysis are not exclusive to their paired works, and the approaches explored in conjunction with one play can certainly be applied to other works with fruitful results. A historical sociolinguistic approach to *shall* works well for *Coriolanus*, for example, because of the overt attention that the term *shall* receives in the play. However, the approach can work equally well on other early modern works, Shakespearean and otherwise. Similarly, as I discuss in greater detail in the chapters that follow, there are inherent and sometimes extensive overlaps among the various approaches featured in the book. Discourse analysis can easily be (and often is) understood as a subset of pragmatics; the matter of language change inflects the discussion of grammar in Chapter 4. The separation of these approaches, while contrived, is useful in teasing out unique and disparate features and tools for analysis. Similarly, the plays discussed in this book represent only a sample of Shakespeare's language. In selecting them, I was mindful of including a range of genres and composition dates, but they are meant to serve as case studies rather than representative works.

Chapter 1, '*Coriolanus*: "Mark you / His absolute 'shall'?"' is focused on the distinctive category of modal verbs, which were in transition in early modern English. Originally main verbs that could occur alone in a clause, the modals gradually became grammaticalized, moving away from their position as primary verbs to act as auxiliaries. The sixteenth century in particular witnessed a significant evolution in the semantic and grammatical application of modal verbs. During this transitional period, the modals retained remnants of their lexical meanings while simultaneously fulfilling a grammatical function. The modals of Shakespeare's time, with their lingering notional meanings, were therefore more fluid than their contemporary counterparts; this category of verbs is emblematic of the language change that separates Shakespeare's language from our own. An understanding of the nuanced differences between present-day modal auxiliaries and those employed by Shakespeare affect our interpretation from everything to 'the literal sense of a passage' to 'the messages that grammatical choices can also convey about the stylistic level of a scene, the tone of a dialogue, or the social status of a character' (Adamson, 'Understanding Shakespeare's Grammar' 211). In *Coriolanus, shall* emerges as a potent and contested word that both subtly and overtly informs the moments of aggressive linguistic encounter that characterize this play. With its strong associations of duty, compulsory action and linguistic control, *shall* proves to be a sought-after prize in the competitive and antagonistic Roman context in which *Coriolanus* is set. Using the lens of language change and historical sociolinguistics, this chapter considers the ways that *shall* embodies questions of authority and control, for the struggle to speak this potent word is here bound up with the capacity to determine future outcomes. In *Coriolanus*, the fate of those who are permitted to 'speak, speak' (1.1.2) is established in large-scale linguistic collisions. I analyse in detail the most prominent example, the 'absolute shall' scene that opens Act Three, in which Coriolanus rails against the tribunes' impudent use of a powerful word from which they are presumably debarred.

Chapter 2, '*Troilus and Cressida*: "Do you think I will?"' provides an outline of the methods and benefits of discourse analysis. It offers an overview of how this methodology has been applied in Shakespeare studies, presents the potential drawbacks of this approach, and suggests why it has posed problems for literary critics. *Troilus and Cressida*, a play in which dialogue is consistently held up as fraught, counterproductive, and working at cross purposes, provides a pertinent case study for discourse analysis. The shared nature of language is resisted at every turn by the play's speakers, and the climate of war and futility that undergirds its action also infuses its dialogue. Extending the discussion of modal verbs introduced in Chapter 1, this chapter explores the polysemy of the word *will* as a suggestive indicator of future outcome and inclination. *Will* becomes a touchstone in *Troilus and Cressida* that is emblematic of the negotiations of control at work in linguistic exchanges in the play. Further, the methods of discourse analysis – including an examination of turn-taking strategies, and assessing the types of utterances produced by speakers – reveal a more complex depiction of the character of Cressida than is often allowed in traditional criticism of the play.

Chapter 3, '*Richard II*: "Here, cousin"' focuses on pragmatics, which considers implicit and contextually sensitive meanings in speech; for example, it uses linguistic terms such as modes of address, and deictic markers with pragmatic import such as *I, now, here, this*. A pragmatic analysis of *Richard II*, with an emphasis on deictic markers and grammatical modes of self-reference, illuminates the protective strategies afforded by language in moments of crisis. King Richard's use of *here* and *this*, in addition to other deictic indicators, demonstrates his subtle bids to retain signifiers of agency and identity (his crown, his land, his power) even as they are being stripped away. The unstable context of *Richard II* renders it an apt subject for deictic analysis, for its action takes place in a context in which the parameters of social power are being redrawn before our eyes. Because the system of deixis works to anchor speakers in a particular setting, it is a particularly fitting mode of analysis to monitor how speakers respond to such fluctuation. In the first part of the chapter, I examine deictic markers of nominal reference, such as personal pronouns and honorifics. These are a particularly revealing type of common word that inscribe both inner state and social rank. The mundane words used for self-positioning have much to convey about the shifting social ground, and they also carry valuable information about the internal perceptions and motivations of speakers. In the second part of the chapter, I turn towards questions of personal stance with a closer analysis of Richard's language. I explore how ritualized language (so often rooted in the body, and always heavily dependent on the position – both physical and social – of the speaker) is transformed in the play, and how Richard uses it to retain some agency even as he is stripped of his modes of self-positioning. Extending the lens of deictic analysis, I suggest that Richard uses the language of the body in order to carve out a space where he is protected from encroaching external influence.

Chapter 4, '*As You Like It*: Much virtue in "if"', takes as its starting point the broad early modern category of grammar. While the term 'grammar' today has a limited range of associations, in Shakespeare's England grammar was a capacious category: it could refer to an array of practices, from the study of Latin, the vernacular, or foreign languages; to translation, etymology and language use in general. This chapter explores how Shakespeare engaged with various aspects of grammar in *As You Like It*, from the transmuted experiences of the Tudor grammar school and the ubiquitous *Lily's Grammar* to experimentation with the profoundly variable lynchpin word 'if'. With its capacity to invoke imagined, hoped-for, or otherwise unreal worlds, 'if' is exceptionally salient to drama. A recognition of the wide influence of grammar, alongside an analysis of a key grammatical term, helps to highlight the possibilities for 'grammar play' in *As You Like It*.

1

Coriolanus: 'Mark you / His absolute "shall"?'

The first moments of Shakespeare's final tragedy, *Coriolanus*, initiate its audience into a dramatic world preoccupied with language. The opening scene, unusually boisterous for Shakespeare, captures the clamour of 'a company of mutinous Citizens' in a pivotal moment of solidarity, as they collectively abandon the fruitless tactic of 'talking' in favour of the more effective avenue of directed action:

> 1 CITIZEN
> Before we proceed any further, hear me speak.
> ALL
> Speak, speak.
> 1 CITIZEN
> You are all resolved rather to die than to famish?
> ALL
> Resolved, resolved.
> 1 CITIZEN
> First, you know Caius Martius is chief enemy to the people.
> ALL
> We know't, we know't.

1 CITIZEN
>Let us kill him, and we'll have corn at our own price.
>Is't a verdict?

ALL
>No more talking on't. Let it be done. Away, away!

(*Cor* 1.1.1–10)

With this exchange, a disparity between speakers that will be maintained and exploited over the course of the play is powerfully introduced.[1] On one hand, the dominant noise belongs to the starving and querulous mob, whose chanted words seem unhinged from typical interactive and communicative functions. The clipped, doubled words acquire an incantatory quality more in line with extra-linguistic sounds than with elements of dialogue. Yet even in the midst of this collective cry, a countering force emerges. Out of the din rises the articulate and enlivening voice of the First Citizen, clarifying and directing the sound of the multitude. The result is a curious confluence of verbal styles; the mob's chanting is offset by a discrete voice, so that two systems of language – the excited babble of a group and the exhortative voice of an orator – collide. The pattern of competing voices that is established here is repeated throughout the play, and the various implications of 'voice' provide a potent subtext.[2] The mob's racket provides a visceral signal of the warring voices that will populate the play, and the words of the individual citizens that emerge from the uproar reinforce the point. There is an early, marked emphasis on the conflict between command and resistance, especially in regard to permitted speech.[3] Almost immediately, the citizens disagree about what they can and cannot say about Caius Martius:

ALL
>Nay, but speak not maliciously.

1 CITIZEN
>I say unto you, what he hath done famously, he did it
>to that end.

> Though soft-conscienced man can be content to say it was for his country, he did it to please his mother, and to be partly proud – which he is, even to the altitude of his virtue.
>
> 2 CITIZEN
> What he cannot help in his nature, you account a vice in him. You must in no way say he is covetous.
>
> 1 CITIZEN
> If I must not, I need not be barren of accusations. He hath faults, with surplus, to tire in repetition.
> (1.1.33–41)

As this first scene establishes, what is spoken and what is not said are of paramount importance, subject to the dictates of the commanding *must*. The point is cemented soon afterwards as the tribunes isolate what they deem the most telling aspect of Caius Martius's behaviour:

> BRUTUS
> Marked you his lip and eyes?
>
> SICINIUS
> Nay, but his taunts.
> (1.1.249–50)

Coriolanus's earliest lesson is the injunction to pay attention to words. The first scene demonstrates the range and impact of different 'voices' that are variously discrete, collective, acquiescent and resistant. The fundamentally communal nature of language – its status as a 'common' resource – is a feature both emphasized and resisted in the play. Instructions governing its appropriate use are rampant, its content cannot be agreed upon, and it is understood to be at once vital and maddeningly ineffectual: the prevailing compulsion to 'speak, speak' is countered by the suspicion that all of this talk only gets in the way of any real action. The First Citizen's protest of 'why stay we prating here?' (1.1.43) seems the natural response to a milieu in which so many voices – the 'multitudinous tongue' so loathed by Coriolanus (3.1.157) – are forced to coexist. And the confused and desirous cry to 'speak' is threaded through all of the action that unfolds over the next five acts. The sparring voices that open the play stay with us; using language to silence language, the mob's 'voice' paradoxically suggests that immediate action, not further talk, is the only appropriate response.

The disquieting possibility that talk is futile haunts the play, but in spite of this risk the speakers of *Coriolanus* take their voices very seriously. They demonstrate a keen awareness of the power of their voices both as an individual force and as capable of collective impact. As they debate Coriolanus's suitability for the consulship and their own role in granting him the position, the citizens acknowledge the discrepancy between individual and collective wants:

1 CITIZEN
Once, if he do require our voices, we *ought* not to deny him.

2 CITIZEN
We *may*, sir, if we *will*.

(2.3.1–3; emphasis added)

The modal verbs in this exchange are worth lingering over, for they represent a rich category of 'common' quotidian words that early modern dramatists like Shakespeare could mine for their associational stores. The modal verbs – *can, could, may, might, will, would, shall, should* and *must* – codify a system that allows speakers to articulate the actions of promising, threatening, commanding, predicting and questioning. Speakers use modals to express things such as permission and prediction, but these verbs also indicate a speaker's stance towards the conditions of their speech. Because modality points to the many ways in which speakers can temper or qualify their messages, it encodes speakers' attitudes towards what they are saying and towards the audience that they are addressing. In fact, in 'pragmatically convey[ing] strong speaker-centred meanings' (Fitzmaurice, 'Tentativeness and Insistence' 17), the modal verbs represent one of the few ways that a speaker's self-positioning is grammaticalized, incorporated into the very structure of the language. It makes sense, then, that moments of interpersonal conflict (in 'actual' and literary language alike) often hinge on modal expressions. In a quantitative study of grammatical modality in early modern English drama, Hugh Craig describes the elevated proportion of modal verbs in tragedies, and he notes that *Coriolanus* has one of the highest counts of all. Craig asserts that the proliferation of modals can be traced to the play's preoccupation with 'tussles of will' and 'the applying and resisting of social leverage', the intersubjective jousting that the modals tend to enact: 'the difficult relations between the individual will and the world, the tragic misfit between the two, are the special territory of *Coriolanus*, and the modals play a considerable part in articulating this struggle' (45).

In asserting that 'We may, sir, if we will,' the Second Citizen succinctly draws out the tensions among social duty (encoded in the First Citizen's *ought*), political power (we *may*), and personal desire (if we *will*). *Ought* occupies a specialized modal territory in that it denotes obligation and logical necessity, but is 'less categorical' than *must* (Quirk 102); it effectively leaves room for doubt and the possibility of doing otherwise (perhaps according to the inclinations of personal will). Indeed, the Second Citizen's reply captures this ambivalence, and it illustrates the nuances of modal ambiguity, suggesting how modal verbs can support a broad network of interpretation. *May* is particularly open to various readings because it can signal motives as varied as simple possibility to strong inclination, permission, or ability. Here, 'we may' could carry the sense of possibility (expressing the potential for two future outcomes that it is within the citizens' ability to carry out: Coriolanus might be denied, or might not be), but it could also have the force of permission or authority to carry out, a connotation that is reinforced by the volitional *will* that follows. The Third Citizen's rejoinder – 'We have power in ourselves to do it, but it is a power that we have no power to do' (2.3.4–5) – reinforces the dilemmas suggested by the modal verbs of the First and Second Citizens. The 'power' they possess is unstable and contingent. The exchange among the citizens illustrates how *Coriolanus* demands attention to the conditions governing the use of modal expressions, and monitors the resounding implications of deploying them in dialogue. In this case, *may* acts as a rebuttal to the dictating *ought*, and the exchange reiterates the familiar dilemma of the plebeian voices; they possess the free choice to follow their own wills, but each expression of will must contend with other individual expressions of will, and, failing to reach consensus, they risk cancelling one another out.[4]

Whereas in present-day English words like *shall* and *will* are essentially formally variants (in most dialects, few conditions remain under which one and not the other is appropriate) this was not the case in early modern English usage. English grammarians since William Lily – who puzzles over whether to define these curious specimens, unknown in Latin, as 'sygnes' before the verb or as verbs in their own right – have faced enormous difficulty in categorizing the 'disarmingly complex' modal verbs (Cummings, *Literary Culture* 428). Originally main lexical verbs that could occur alone in a clause, the modals underwent a long process of grammaticalization, moving away from their position as primary verbs in Old English to auxiliary verbs in present-day English.[5] During this transitional period, modals retained remnants of their lexical meanings while simultaneously fulfilling a grammatical function. The period concurrent with Shakespeare's lifetime falls squarely within this time of transition, so that the modal verbs used by speakers in Shakespeare's England had lingering non-auxiliary features that gave them the potential for a wider range of meaning than they have today. Consider an exchange between Hamlet and Horatio as they discuss the ghostly visit of Old Hamlet:

HAMLET
 I would I had been there.

HORATIO
 It would have much amazed you.

(*Ham* 1.2.232–3)

Here, Hamlet's *would* functions primarily as a lexical verb indicating desire, a usage that is no longer available to English speakers in most dialects. Horatio's *would*, however, has a notably different function, with a modal application akin to the *would have* construction in present-day English, which acts as a hypothetical marker of prediction. The close proximity of the two *would*s within this verbal exchange draws attention to their divergent functions and meanings.

While the modal verbs in present-day English still retain a flavour of their old semantic influence – there is a discernible difference, for example, in the degree of commitment and obligation between 'he shall return tomorrow' and 'he will return tomorrow' – they are more readily transposable today than they were in Shakespeare's time. For Shakespeare's speakers, the non-auxiliary features brought much to bear on the choice between *shall* and *will* in linguistic expressions of the future, for the original lexical associations – *will* with Old English *willan*, meaning 'wish' or 'desire', *shall* with Old English *sceal*, denoting obligation – strongly informed these terms even in their auxiliary roles. It was only at the beginning of the eighteenth century that *will* shed its lexical sense of wishing or desiring, and that *shall* could convey a 'purely temporal reference to future time'.[6] The result of the modal instability in early modern English is that the pragmatic effect of Shakespeare's *shall*s and *will*s is not quite equivalent to the effect of those verbs in present-day English. Consider two similar lines in Shakespeare's sonnets: 'Loving offenders, thus I will excuse ye' (42.5), and 'But love, for love, thus shall excuse my jade' (51.12). While the core meaning of these lines would be maintained even if the modal verbs were transposed, a key set of associations would be lost. The *will* in the former line bears shades of willingness and yearning not present in the *shall* of the latter, which denotes a more forcefully mandated vision of the future. In a work as invested in the subtle power of the poet's words as Shakespeare's sonnets, the nuances that these verbs afford are of considerable interest.

An appreciation of these nuances is the unique reward of a historical linguistic approach. Because historical linguistics is broadly concerned with language change over time, it helps to illuminate differences between various periods in the development of a language. This type of insight is vital in exploring a word like *shall*, which has undergone significant changes during and since Shakespeare's lifetime. Because the *shall*s of Shakespeare's age were laden with potential meaning, a historical perspective helps to unveil the rich associational stores that Shakespeare and his contemporaries could draw upon when using this word. Historical sociolinguistics retains the focus on language change, but with an eye towards language in use: 'Because no language evolves in a social vacuum, the speakers of earlier English should not be ignored when their language is looked at through the telescope of historical linguistics' (Nevalainen 2). More broadly, sociolinguistics considers the context of interaction, 'language as it is constructed and co-constructed, shaped and re-shaped, in the discourse of everyday life, and as it reflects and creates the social realities of that life' (Machan and Scott v). Because it focuses on language as a site of collaboration, sociolinguistics is useful in highlighting the ways that power and identity are negotiated. The expansive, interdisciplinary field of sociolinguistics is certainly not a monolith; debates flourish about where sociolinguists should direct their attention, and which methodologies they should employ. Yet for literary critics – particularly those interested in the dialogue-driven genre of drama – aspects of recent work in sociolinguistics are promising. Dialogue is where power is negotiated, where identity is established, where relationships are tested and maintained. The sociolinguistic emphasis on dialogue is a natural fit for the analysis of dramatic language, which fundamentally depends on the conflict and negotiation embedded in dialogue.

Historical sociolinguistics thus has a dual emphasis: it considers the linguistic features of past periods of the language but always treats them as fundamentally entwined with social context, rather than as isolated phenomena. The goal of an historical sociolinguistic analysis is not simply an identification of traits or features of past language use, but rather an understanding of how these features operated within their social environments. How might the conditions of speech affect usage? What role do factors such as relative power, status, gender, or control play in the development and deployment of linguistic features? Of course, studies of dialogue and conversation from past periods are different from contemporary ones. Modern sociolinguistics makes use of oral sources and spoken language, while historical sociolinguistics relies on written accounts of spoken language (often in documents such as trial transcripts). This is another reason why dramatic works are well suited to this type of analysis. As a written representation of speech – albeit artistic rather than actual – dramatic dialogue offers us a glimpse of historical speech that is otherwise lost to us. Moreover, because it combines linguistic function (the grammatical marking of future time) with social implications (the applying and resisting of social pressure and leverage) *shall* is particularly well suited to a sociolinguistic analysis. When we appreciate the subtle differences between present-day modal auxiliaries and those employed by Shakespeare, we can better understand everything from 'the literal sense of a passage' to 'the messages that grammatical choices can also convey about the stylistic level of a scene, the tone of a dialogue, or the social status of a character' (Adamson 'Understanding Shakespeare's Grammar' 211).

The respective associations of *shall* and *will* with obligation and volition during their initial transition to a modal auxiliary function forced many early grammarians into a rather shaky prescriptivist framework. Hypothesizing that volition was less easily projected to other people than obligation and necessity – and, conversely, that a true expression of volition can be made only by the agent of that will – seventeenth-century grammarians such as Bishop John Wallis (1653) proposed a set of rules whereby *shall* in the first person simply indicates a prediction, whereas *will* is used for promising or threatening. In the second and third persons the reverse is true (based on the supposition that it is less common for a speaker to state his or her own obligation) so that *shall* signals a promise or a threat while *will* serves simply to predict (Arnovick 2; Rissanen 202). While evidence from actual usage does not always bear out these patterns, the very existence of the so-called Wallis Rules highlights several important elements of these modal expressions. First, their puzzling nature has provoked an anxious reaction in language pundits from the very beginning; they are renegade words that do not fit neatly into an orderly system, and they are perhaps all the more troubling because they encode the socially loaded issues of desire and obligation. Second, their semantic weight has substantial currency in their usage; *shall* and *will* are not simply alternate indicators of future time, but significant choices which express a speaker's stance. As this assessment shows, and as the existence of the Wallis rules demonstrate, the pragmatic intentions of the speaker matter a great deal to the meaning of the chosen modal verb. The Wallis system 'poses the future auxiliary in relation to the speaker of the utterance rather than the grammatical subject of the sentence' (Arnovick 9), thereby making central the experience of the speaker to the force the utterance. The indistinct boundary between the grammatical field of future time and the conceptual realm of modality, which deals in desire and possibility, provides ripe terrain for analysis of speakers' envisioned futures, and indeed of their wider worlds, both private and social.

Given their complexity and wealth of speaker-oriented information, the modals can act as subtly effective poetic flourishes. Modal expressions are by their very nature equivocal and potentially dissembling. Such nuance, particularly as it concerns the persona that one presents to the world, is central to the close reading of literary language. In *Julius Caesar*, when Cassius says, 'Do not presume too much upon my love /

I may do that I shall be sorry for' (4.3.63–4), *may* and *shall* convey a delicious ambiguity – is Cassius issuing a prediction? Voicing a threat? Declaring his own power? The multiple valences of *may* and *shall* represent the best sort of poetic language: suggestive and equivocal. It is no wonder that early modern dramatists such as Shakespeare, alert to the details of dialogue as well as to the power of variously signifying words, regularly draw attention to them. In *King John*, Constance expresses her resistance by asserting, 'Thou mayst, thou shalt; I will not go with thee' (2.2.67). The parallel structure of the line foregrounds the modal verbs, urging listeners to pay attention to the distinctions between them, and to recognize the surprising force of the simple word *will* as an insistent declaration of intention and resistance. When Christopher Marlowe's Tamburlaine hears his ally Theridimas boast of his skill, he expresses his approval for Theridimas's forward-oriented modal choices: 'Well said, Theridimas! speak in that mood; / For Will and Shall best fitteth Tamburlaine' (3.3.40–1). Here, *will* and *shall* encode Tamburlaine's striving nature and his tendency towards definitive action. Early modern poets, too, recognized the potential of these words. The most arresting line of Sonnet 47 in Philip Sidney's *Astrophil and Stella* is a stark, monosyllabic sequence of subject and verb: 'I may, I must, I can, I will, I do.' This series of vows reads like an excerpt from a grammar school textbook, but it also exemplifies the speaker's bids for control. Astophil's modal expressions here are revealing; not only do modal verbs provide insight into speaker agency, they also offer evidence of a speakers' perceptions of themselves and of the world, incorporating social factors such as relative power, affinity, affection and politeness. It is these pragmatic elements that have traditionally given grammarians pause. It is not enough to think of modal verbs merely as function words signalling notions such as permission and command, for they also encode a range of additional interpersonal meanings and are central to the dynamics of human communication. The subtleties that render the modals unwieldy for grammarians are the very features that make these words so compelling for writers, and illuminating for literary critics.

As a potent indicator of social positioning, *shall* linguistically inscribes power relations, traces speaker expectations, and illuminates and insists on specific rules of social interaction. Such a word carries particular resonance in the conflict-focused milieu of drama, and especially in a play such as *Coriolanus*, which showcases the tension between civic duty, familial authority and responsibility, and personal ambition: '*Shall* expresses aspects of obligation and desire, and therefore showcases the boundary between the demands of a speaker's public world and the wishes of his private one' (Bybee, Perkins, and Pagliuca 262). From the earliest beginnings of English literature, expressions of obligation and power in the spirit of present-day *shall* have been difficult to translate with precision. Bede's *Ecclesiastical History of the English People*, completed in 731, contains one of the earliest examples of English poetry, 'Caedmon's Hymn'. The devotional poem opens with an exhortation to worship God and to acknowledge his work of creation: 'Nu sculon herian heofonrices weard / Metodes meahta ond his modgeþanc, / weorc wuldorfaeder, swa he wundra gehwaes, / ece Drihten, or astealde' (Now we ought to praise the Heaven-kingdom's guardian, / the Maker's might and his mind's thoughts, / the work of the glory-father, as he of each of wonders, / eternal Lord, established a beginning) (Black et al. 23). The initiatory *sculon* is an anchor word here, providing the poem's first hard stress as well as its first instance of assonance. This Old English verb is rooted in Indo-European *skel* and Proto-Germanic *skulan*, with connotations of obligation and necessity. Indeed, different translations of 'Caedmon's Hymn' use a variety of present-day English terms to capture *sculon*'s effect: 'Now we ought to praise'; 'Now we shall praise'; 'Now we must praise.' While each translation conveys the same sense of obligation – and the particularly strict commitment that accompanies religious practice – the nuances of each term differ. 'Must' is a starker injunction than 'ought'; 'ought' points to an extrinsic motivation while 'should' suggests a more intrinsic one. As this earliest instance of English poetry demonstrates, the meanings of *shall*'s predecessors – which include *sculon* and *sceal* – are slippery. *Shall*'s lineage, steeped in relative power and obligation, is suggestive of deep ties to social status, its etymological history anchored in notions of wrongdoing and repayment:

> *he sceal* ... may have been something like *he has done something* (probably committed an offense or a crime) in consequence of which he now (OE) *is scyldig* ... When *he sceal* came to be combined with an infinitive ... it expressed what the person denoted by the subject had to do, *owed to do*, was obliged to do. (Arnovick 10; emphasis in original)

The implication that a person 'was liable of debt, [and] had to pay' (Fachinetti 117) was how the association of modern *shall* with futurity first came about; in order to repay the debt, the person at whom this verb was directed had to carry out a future action. As these origins suggest, *shall* is a forceful word which harnesses a specialized semantic legacy, one shadowed by disparate power and required action. The deployment of *shall* can sometimes serve as a kind of social grenade, exposing the dynamics of power between speakers and demanding that some action be effected. By using a modal expression such as *shall*, thereby suggesting or insisting that one is obliged to do something, a speaker impinges on another's wish for autonomy and suggests that his or her power supersedes that of the interlocutor.[7] Social power and positioning are central to the successful application of modal expressions; those who possess relative power are apt to be less inhibited in their expressions of obligation and desire, just as they are less likely to soften these threatening words. Conversely, those with relatively little power are more prone to compliance and the concealment of their own desires. *Shall* naturally tends to recur in the dialogue of powerful characters; it scarcely needs noting that Shakespeare's kings employ obligation-*shall* quite liberally. In Shakespeare's time, *shall* bore strong traces of predestination or infallible decree; the result of this lingering association is that *shall* seemed to appeal to a force greater than one's own will, a specialized type of authority afforded gods, monarchs, and (in the case of *Coriolanus*) overbearing mothers.[8]

Of the many conspicuous instances of modal usage in *Coriolanus, shall*, the commanding modal marker of obligation, is given the most prominent attention. Its double function as both indicator of resistant desire and marker of the social order lends *shall* a distinctive force in this play, and tracking its use uncovers compelling patterns of coercion and insistence. *Shall* – particularly in early modern English – is a forceful word which harnesses a specialized semantic legacy, one characterized by disparate power and required action. In other words, the defining feature of *shall* usage is the belief that one's own words can bring about a future outcome: it is not merely hoped for, but actively sought and enacted through language. As a word that designates a speaker's capacity to bring about some future action, *shall* may be held up as a lexical prize to be claimed. In these exchanges, the 'victor' who lays claim to *shall* sees his or her intention for the future fulfilled. It thus seems the natural modal choice for the domineering Volumnia, who can frequently be heard telling others what they *shall* do. In an early exchange, a familiar battle of wills between mother and daughter-in-law, which embodies the tension between personal desire and social obligation, turns on their modal choices:

VALERIA
  Come, lay aside your stitchery. I *must* have you play the idle housewife with me this afternoon.

VIRGILIA
  No, good madam. I *will* not out of doors.

VALERIA
  Not out of doors?

VOLUMNIA
  She *shall*, she *shall*.

VIRGILIA
   Indeed no, by your patience. I'*ll* not over the threshold
   till my lord return from the wars.

VALERIA
   Fie, you confine yourself most unreasonably. Come, you
   must go visit the good lady that lies in.

VIRGILIA
   I *will* wish her speedy strength, and visit her with my
   prayers, but I *cannot* go thither.

VOLUMNIA
   Why, I pray you?

VIRGILIA:
   'Tis not to save labour, nor that I want love.

VALERIA
   You *would* be another Penelope. Yet they say all the yarn
   she spun in Ulysses' absence did but fill Ithaca full of
   moths. Come, I *would* your cambric were sensible as
   your finger, that you *might* leave pricking it for pity.
   Come, you *shall* go with us.

VIRGILIA
   No, good madam, pardon me, indeed I *will* not forth.
                         (*Cor* 1.3.71–90; emphasis added)

Virgilia couches her refusal in deferential modal language; she places the emphasis on her own volition and even inability, repeating that she '*will* not out of doors' and '*cannot* go thither' to which Volumnia responds with firm insistence: 'she *shall*, she *shall*'. This passage shows how modality inscribes boundaries of relationships and relative social power. Volumnia capitalizes on her rank as Coriolanus's mother and Virgilia's elder in her conviction that her wishes take precedence; her modals of obligation stand in sharp contrast to Virgilia's more tempered choices. Virgilia is shrewd enough to recognize that deploying a *shall* of her own against Volumnia could be too inflammatory to be effective, and she chooses instead simply to stand resolute. There is, however, a subdued escalation in the force of Virgilia's modal verbs from the weaker 'I will not', which emphasizes her own volition, to 'I cannot', which suggests less agency and accountability; Virgilia appeals to the illusion that she is not only unwilling but in fact unable to leave. She closes the discussion with the strongest statement in her arsenal: 'No, at a word, madam. Indeed I must not. I wish you much mirth' (1.3.111–12). Her modal choices here map a trajectory from personal desire to social obligation; the emphasis is shifted from the impetus of her own desire to more nebulous dicta – she 'must' not leave according to the mandates for a decorous wife, which here trump Volumnia's authority as implacable mother-in-law. Echoes of Volumnia's 'She shall, she shall' recur throughout the play, and this unremitting battle of *shall* pivots on who is permitted to impose this command and who is compelled to heed it.

Volumnia's commanding language, largely devoid of niceties and peppered with imperatives, exposes her understanding of her own social position. Her modal expressions are the understated engines of her dictatorial speech, asserting her rank and insinuating control over future outcomes. Even at the nadir of her influence, after Coriolanus has been banished, she retains the potential to vanquish with a word. Confronted with her wailing presence, Brutus and Sicinius appear fearful – 'Let's not meet her ... They say she's mad' (4.2.7–9) – and Menenius implores her to 'be not so loud' (4.2.12). Volumnia's response to the enemy tribunes is telling: 'If that I could for weeping, you should hear – Nay, and you shall hear some' (4.2.15–16). Here, Volumnia pushes the authoritative potential of *shall* to its limits; she does not simply impinge on the tribunes' autonomy, but instead openly declares her own goal to quash that very freedom, revising her tempered aim that they '*should* hear' – like *ought*, *should* is a less categorical marker of necessity – to the stronger '*shall*'. Cummings argues that while *shall* necessarily signifies action taking place in the future, 'in practice it is often difficult to distinguish this from an obligation or an undertaking' (*Literary Culture* 215).

Volumnia exploits this ambiguity, and coming from her lips, the word acquires the flavour of divine edict – less a statement about what is going to transpire than a fierce guarantee.

Shall statements tend to act as threats or promises, and they carry the force of obligation and unyielding personal intention, regardless of the wishes of the addressee. Predictably, Coriolanus employs them regularly: 'Hence, rotten thing, or I shall shake thy bones / Out of thy garments' (3.1.178–9); 'He that retires, I'll take him for a Volsce, / And he shall feel mine edge' (1.4.29–30), or for his rival Aufidius to relish the promise of continued battles: ''Tis sworn between us we shall ever strike / Till one can do no more' (1.2.35–6). Because they stake out the conditions of the future according to the strong intention of the speaker, *I* and *we shall* statements are an effective rhetorical tactic for an intimidating foe. Yet in the milieu of *Coriolanus*, where so many voices freely and antagonistically declare their intentions, speakers often find themselves corralled in the public arena of warring threats and promises. Ironically, then, the *I shall* usage can also point to a sort of declaration of circumscribed agency, an appeal that one's hands are tied. A mild version of this *I shall* construction occurs in the first words spoken by Cominius in the play, as he is called upon to recount Coriolanus's achievements: 'I shall lack voice' (2.2.80). His promise that he will be unable to communicate adequately Coriolanus's feats (a fear that resonates with the play's concerns about the relative power of 'voices') concedes a sort of helplessness, albeit a trivial sort that taps in to the conventional *topos* of praise for a valiant leader. A more serious expression of powerlessness occurs shortly after Cominius's admission, as Coriolanus reluctantly agrees to show his wounds to the people as he appeals for their votes: 'It is a part / That I shall blush in acting, and might well / Be taken from the people' (2.2.143–4). Like Virgilia in her refusal of Volumnia, Coriolanus makes it clear that his intentions are not a matter of choice – just as Virgilia 'cannot' leave her home, Coriolanus couches his shame in the language of obligation. The *I shall* conveys a sense of necessity, and confirms that Coriolanus agrees to it not as a matter of will, but of compliance. The requirements of others ensure that his back is against the wall, with no exit in sight. As Sicinius asserts in equally insistent modal terms, 'Sir, the people / Must have their voices' (2.2.138–9).

The framework of modal analysis puts one of the defining moments of *Coriolanus*, Menenius's telling of the fable of the belly, into new focus. Drawing on the common metaphor of a citizenry as part of one larger body – in his infamous and poorly received account, the patricians are the belly and the plebeians the 'great toe' (1.1.150) – Menenius speaks of the community as an organic whole, each member a cell in the larger common organism with a mandate to 'mutually participate … minister / Unto the appetite and affection common / Of the whole body' (1.1.98–100). The concept of modality runs counter to such a self-denying ideal, for by definition it gives voice to self-interest. What the system of modal verbs shows us 'is the way that the speaker's attitude of volition and expectation is formally represented' (Arnovick 6). Despite Menenius's vision of unity, grammatical modality lays bare the potential for each person to be a 'mutinous part' (1.1.94) with desires all his own.

With its relentless focus on the tensions between individual will and collective duty, and its antagonistic central figure, *Coriolanus* offers an ideal case study for the analysis of modality in action. The play's bullying protagonist, initially named Caius Martius, appears onstage with fighting words: 'Hang 'em!'; 'Go get you home, you fragments!'; 'What's the matter, you dissentious rogues?' (1.1.185, 218, 159). Caius Martius Coriolanus has often been accused of lacking the linguistic verve, introspective querying and desperate personal turmoil so fundamental to other protagonists in early modern tragedy. Yet language in use is consistently held up for attention in the play, most apparently in the play's engagements with social communication and negotiation and competing linguistic communities. Coriolanus himself is a key figure in a language-based analysis of the play as an active participant in and manipulator of its networks of communication. He purports to stand alone and repeatedly declares his mistrust of words, fashioning himself as a soldier whose skill on the battlefield does not extend to the world of public life and communication: 'When blows have made me stay, I fled from words' (2.2.70). At the same time, he establishes himself as an astute reader of the linguistic rules that govern dialogue in the play, and the skill that he consistently demonstrates in a wide array of speech situations suggests that he is neither as reticent nor as inscrutable as has sometimes been suggested. Coriolanus is, in fact, one of Shakespeare's most talkative characters, speaking 'one quarter of the play's 3200 lines, a part larger than any in the tragedies except for Hamlet, Iago, and Othello' (McDonald, 52). Additionally, while the war-bred soldier 'ill-schooled / In bolted language' (3.1.323–4) rarely speaks alone onstage, and tends not to engage in the self-revealing rhetoric of Shakespeare's renowned soliloquists, he reveals a great deal in his conversations. The bulk of his words are spoken in interactive dialogue, using the seemingly mundane lynchpins of common communication. Yet these simple words also encode clues about a speaker's self-positioning, and they provide proof that there are many means of tracing linguistic subjectivity in drama. Decisions, quarrels, questions: such processes hinge on the ordinary function words of the language. Moreover, Coriolanus's vigilant attention to the details of dialogue consistently results in identifying and railing against any perceived violation. Words deemed by him to be bold or defiant – 'shall' (3.1.91); 'traitor' (3.3.66); 'boy' (5.6.105) – are subject to his public scrutiny and scorn. These censorious lessons serve to tell us something important about Coriolanus: he knows how social language works and he is sensitive to the power contained in single words.

The clashing desires and obligations of the assortment of characters – citizens, tribunes, patricians – produce evident friction in the modal expressions that convey the respective impulses of duty and desire. Often the effect is subtle, as when characters alternate between *shall* and *will* and thus showcase the distinctions between the two. The private exchanges between Brutus and Sicinius, discussions that tend to focus on bids for power, frequently convey this tension:

SICINIUS
    I wish no better
    Than have him hold that purpose and to put it
    In execution.

BRUTUS
    'Tis most like he will.

SICINIUS
    It shall be to him then as our good wills,
    A sure destruction.

                                                        (2.1.233–7)

The modals of this passage are discreetly emphasized; in terms of form, the line breaks place stress on *will* (as well as the juxtaposed, line opening *shall*), while the dialogue highlights Shakespeare's familiar wordplay with *will*, drawing on various senses of the word and underscoring its status as both a verb of intention and a noun of volition. Indeed, 'our good wills' reads as ambiguous – it recalls the positive association of the noun 'goodwill', but more prominently *will* enacts a modal function as the verb modifying 'good'. The meaning thus becomes *as our advantage ('good') requires ('wills')*, thereby attributing intention and necessity to the 'good' or 'benefit' of the tribunes, an anthropomorphizing verbal trick that strengthens their claim against Coriolanus. The *shall* inserted closely between the two instances of *will* further underscores the word's modal function. The effect of this sequence is that the hostile 'will' of Coriolanus is first pitted against the self-styled 'good wills' of the tribunes, then virtually dismissed by the requirement ('will') of that collective 'good', and further cancelled out by the powerful *shall* of the tribunes that follows it. The *shall* thus encodes the perceived capacity of Brutus and Sicinius to subdue the antagonistic 'will' of Coriolanus.

A similar scenario unfolds in the crucial scene in which Volumnia chastises her son for railing against the people, and goads him to defer to the wishes of the tribunes and plebeians. Coriolanus's verbs depict his reluctant stance as a product of inability rather than will; when urged to 'repent what you have spoke' (3.2.37), he retreats – like Virgilia in her own face-off with Volumnia – to an expression of ability and permission rather than volition: 'For them? I cannot do it to the gods; / Must I then do't to them?' (38–9). Like all modal verbs, *can* is polysemous, and its various meanings often shade into one another. Besides the connotation of 'ability', *can* may also represent, among other things, possibility and permission. In this example, Coriolanus moves away from values associated with his subjective state (such as his volition) in order to emphasize a lack of agency. According to his modal choices – 'cannot'; 'must' – his capacity to 'repent' is largely attributable to an external source apart from his realm of control. Volumnia's remonstration is methodical and canny. She first attempts to sway him by emphasizing that this deferral of will is exactly the point, proposing that he disregard volition in favour of basic ability:

> Because that now it lies you on to speak
> To th' people, not by your own instruction,
> Nor by th' matter which your heart prompts you,
> But with such words that are but roted in
> Your tongue, though but bastards and syllables
> Of no allowance to your bosom's truth.
>
> (3.2.53–8)

By denouncing rote words as meaningless 'syllables', Volumnia makes it easy for Coriolanus to submit to her prescription for his speech. As Cominius and Menenius prod Coriolanus, Volumnia effectively speaks for him: 'He must and will. / [*to Coriolanus*] Prithee now, say you will and go about it' (3.2.98–9). It is telling that the forceful *must* is buttressed by *will* rather than *shall*, the typical modal of choice in a bid for obedience. Indeed, Volumnia's statement suggests how significant mere 'syllables' can be; her use of 'will' hints that personal volition is more important to her endeavour than she has led her son to believe. She attempts to change Coriolanus's 'bosom's truth', resetting his *own* will to acknowledge the greater prize that lies beyond the simple act of deference. Her goal appears to be consensus rather than acquiescence; despite her claims that the tongue trumps the heart, Volumnia demands evidence that Coriolanus's intentions match her own, if not those of the citizens. Volitional coercion is Volumnia's calling card, the tactic whereby she realizes her power over others. Such a strategy maps the processes by which power is established and disseminated: not only is Volumnia attempting to control Coriolanus's speech in this particular instance, she is also vying to extend that control beyond the immediate linguistic encounter. In a discussion of how power manifests in dialogue, Vimala Herman suggests that 'power in action is power to control consequences of speech, to control the sequels to one's illocutionary acts, and to bend other's actions to one's word and will' (*Dramatic Discourse* 216). In this case, Volumnia's successful outcome marks another triumph for her, for Coriolanus's response mimics his mother's calculated modal choices: 'Must I go show them my unbarbed sconce? / Must I with my base tongue give to my noble heart / A lie that it must bear? Well, I will do't' (3.2.100–102). The articulation of personal desire is one of the most direct means available to a speaker to position and expose himself in the world. Volumnia seems attuned to this reality, aware that changing Coriolanus's will amounts to changing him. And *Coriolanus*, on a wider scale, seems to be preoccupied with the process of this change. Perhaps the strongest expression of altered or confounded will comes from the Third Citizen in the aftermath of Coriolanus's expulsion: 'and though we willingly consented to his banishment, yet it was against our will' (4.6.146–7). This apparent paradox captures a dilemma at the heart of *Coriolanus*: in an environment awash with competing and coercing voices, it is difficult to retain control over one's own will.

Even in a play crowded with verbal skirmishes, the conflicts of Act 3, Scene 1 stand out. The presumed rules governing modal choices are laid bare in an open clash over the right to speak a commanding modal. By exposing the conditions by which a speaker is permitted to employ a future-defining word such as *shall*, the scene makes explicit the transformative processes in which these rules are defined and violated. It further alerts us to Coriolanus's insight: he is aware of the workings of language in action, and of the ways that individual words may be exploited to his benefit or to his disadvantage. Reading this scene with an eye trained on the commonplace words of the exchange and an understanding of the unique grammatical force of *shall* shows how the nuances of grammar are put on display in *Coriolanus*. There is an accent placed on acts of social speech, both in the undercurrent of impending confrontation – the suspense of observing the colliding factions who are bound to argue – and in the patterns of the dialogue itself.

The moments prior to this clash, which feature Coriolanus claiming a powerful linguistic position, serve to accentuate the abrupt shift when he encounters the tribunes. The first words of the scene belong to Coriolanus, who demands details about Aufidius's newly formed army: 'Tullus Aufidius then had made new head?' (3.1.1). His speech continues as an interrogation-style dialogue, in which Coriolanus is the sole questioner. He attempts to pry details about Aufidius from Lartius, and displays a particular interest in what Aufidius has *said*:

CORIOLANUS
Saw you Aufidius? ... Spoke he of me?

LARTIUS
He did, my lord.

CORIOLANUS
How? What?

(3.1.8, 12–14)

The types of questions posed by Coriolanus, used to elicit information, are typical of speakers wishing to take 'an initiatory role' since they serve the various authoritative functions of interrogation, challenging prior talk, and achieving commands (Eggins and Slade 87). The pattern unveiled by these questions is that of a firmly established, rule-bound speech community. Coriolanus is its leader, organizing the parameters of the interaction, constraining the responses of others, and demanding and receiving information in a manner reminiscent of breathless gossip. It sets up Coriolanus not merely as a participant, but rather as the primary controller of a linguistic exchange that highlights the significance of words themselves, the 'how' and 'what' of speech. Given this authoritative display, it is unsurprising that Coriolanus attempts to extend his position as regulator of discourse even when he encounters the antagonistic tribunes.

The scene's visual set-up may remind contemporary audiences of a *High Noon*-style confrontation: a public street in Rome on market day. From stage left, an entourage of proud patricians, led by the harsh and disdainful Coriolanus. From stage right, a pair of scheming tribunes, Brutus and Sicinius, invigorated by the promise of unsettling their haughty adversary. The scene hums with the frisson of impending conflict and the audience watches in suspense as the factions advance, bound to collide. The dramatic intensity of this scene is a characteristic Shakespearean flourish. In Shakespeare's version, unlike in Plutarch's account, the tribunes have already decided to deny Coriolanus the consulship, a significant change in context that heightens their confidence as they approach. The promise of conflict, and of Coriolanus's reaction to such a brazen challenge, is wonderfully realized. While Coriolanus initially takes charge of the dialogue in typical domineering style, initiating an interrogation-style dialogue, he is brought up short by Sicinius's impertinent imperative to 'Pass no further' (3.1.25). Retorting in disgusted surprise, Coriolanus immediately attempts to steer the dialogue back to familiar patterns by regaining his role as sole questioner: 'Ha? What is that? … "What makes this change?"' (3.1.27–8). The situation escalates as the tribunes refuse to 'give way', and even

Coriolanus's supporters implore him to cease: 'not in this heat, sir, now ... No more words, we beseech you' (3.1.64, 77). The clash culminates when Coriolanus, operating under the model that 'his heart's his mouth' (3.1.259), refuses to self-censor, and Sicinius threatens to subdue the 'mind' that communicates its unfiltered thoughts without pause:

SICINIUS
    It is a mind that shall remain a poison
    Where it is, not poison any further.

CORIOLANUS
    'Shall remain'?
    Hear you this Triton of the minnows? Mark you
    His absolute 'shall'?

COMINIUS
    'Twas from the canon.

Coriolanus's response here bears the hallmarks of a speaker familiar and comfortable with authoritative language, one who is attuned to the factors that inform and shape power (linguistic and otherwise). Coriolanus reacts with righteous fury to the tribunes' impertinence. Yet the acquiescence to which he is accustomed is nowhere in sight. Instead, Sicinius pushes back with a threat. By declaring his intention to subdue Coriolanus's 'mind', which communicates its unfiltered thoughts without pause, Sicinius effectively vows to terminate Coriolanus's power of speech:

CORIOLANUS
    'Shall'?
    O good but most unwise patricians, why,
    You grave but reckless senators, have you thus
    Given Hydra here to choose an officer
    That, with his peremptory 'shall', being but
    The horn and noise o'th'monster's, wants not spirit
    To say he'll turn your current in a ditch
    And make your channel his? If he have power,

> Then vail your ignorance; if none, awake
> Your dangerous lenity. If you are learned,
> Be not as common fools; if you are not,
> Let them have cushions by you. You are plebeians,
> If they be senators, and they are no less
> When, both your voices blended, the great'st taste
> Most palates theirs. They choose their magistrate,
> And such a one as he, who puts his 'shall',
> His popular 'shall', against a graver bench
> Than ever frowned in Greece. By Jove himself,
> It makes the consuls base; and my soul aches
> To know, when two authorities are up,
> Neither supreme, how soon confusion
> May enter 'twixt the gap of both and take
> The one by th'other.
>
> (3.1.92–113)

Skilfully constructed, withering and defiant, the speech in every aspect shows Coriolanus's bids for linguistic mastery. Indeed, this response demonstrates his resolute unwillingness to participate in the newly revised linguistic framework aggressively put forth by Sicinius; part of his strategy of rebuffing Sicinius's 'absolute shall' is denying him the privilege of being an interlocutor, for he directs his invective towards the 'grave but reckless senators' rather than the tribunes. Coriolanus's refusal to use his power as addressor to confer acknowledgement on his antagonists – rendering them 'a kind of nothing, titleless' (5.1.13) – is the first strategy by which he attempts to retain linguistic control. As his subsequent speech shows, however, he is ultimately aware that even unacknowledged entities have the distressing capacity to impinge on his agency. It is this double edge – indignation coupled with the suspicion of futility – that makes Coriolanus's attack both brazen as well as curiously poignant and vulnerable. His ire is readily apparent, especially as he condemns Sicinius for his presumptive authority in using *shall*, suggesting that he – a delegate of the mere 'minnows' in the social pond – is impotent to execute it.

Coriolanus's interrogation of the authority behind this word invokes the critical terrain of J.L. Austin and Stanley Fish; in the terminology of speech act theory, Coriolanus objects that Sicinius's *shall* cannot perform as a *shall* because he does not have the requisite influence to speak it.[9] He further takes offence at Sicinius's use of *shall* in such a public denunciatory fashion, demanding that fellow listeners 'mark' his temerity. His invective virtually parses the future-altering, hierarchy-determining modal verb, and his outrage offers an intriguing commentary on social language systems in the play. One of the driving concerns of *Coriolanus* – who is permitted to say what to whom – is here laid bare.

Beneath the fury, though, are hints of burgeoning alarm. Coriolanus's *shall*s in this speech are successively modified by three striking adjectives: 'absolute'; 'peremptory'; and 'popular'. Interestingly, his first target is Sicinius's 'absolute' *shall*; the initial sting, it seems, lies less in the insolence of Sicinius's utterance than in its unequivocal force. His outrage seems natural given that it is typically Coriolanus who is aligned with the absolute; Volumnia's rebuke that he is 'too absolute' (3.2.40) is one of several similar observations throughout the play. Yet his objection also gives voice to anxieties about the very scenario that is being enacted before us: Coriolanus the vocal leader is here stopped short by a usurper seeking the position of privilege in a dialogue. As Coriolanus knows, there can be only one determiner of the 'absolute'; the word's very definition precludes plurality. Sicinius appropriates the very word that denotes the linguistic sovereign, the commanding *shall* that singles him out as one who 'speak[s] o'th'people as if you were a god / To punish, not a man of their infirmity' (3.1.83–4). By robbing him of this word, Sicinius assumes the sovereign position and ensures that Coriolanus take his rightful place alongside the people themselves, rather than as a deity above them. The fear of being subjected to the destructive control of others is further evident in Coriolanus's assessment of 'peremptory shall'. It is worth recalling that 'peremptory' has its etymological roots in the Latin *perimere*, meaning 'to thoroughly destroy', and that this meaning has in a legal sense been transmuted to 'put a decisive end to'.[10] In one sense, Coriolanus's use of this modifier intensifies his argument for the preposterousness of Sicinius's position: it is absurd that Sicinius's self-appointed authority, nothing but the 'horn and noise o'th'monster's', should carry any type of delimiting power. But the flip side of this semblance of absurdity is that it veers into the realm of reality. In this way, the absolute and peremptory *shall*s here deployed by Sicinius provide a grammatical prelude to the pivotal moment when Coriolanus is forced to stave off his own banishment with the counter-declaration to Rome and its inhabitants, 'I banish you' (3.3.122). What at first appears to be simply the railing of a petulant bully against losing his privilege to speak is also a cry for self-preservation. Despite his aggressive claims for the invalid authority of the tribune, Coriolanus recognizes that this 'Triton of the minnows' represents an increasingly absolute threat, for the word that Sicinius wields with such insouciance has the potential to put an end to, to destroy, and (as Coriolanus will soon discover) to send elsewhere. This scene acts as a pivot point – an unraveling begins, as Coriolanus begins to be victimized by the very modes of language that he once used against others.

Given this dawning threat, the ending of Coriolanus's tirade is particularly telling. He closes with an appeal to social order, noting that when competing authorities collide, the result is confusion: 'when two authorities are up, / Neither supreme, how soon confusion / May enter 'twixt the gap of both and take / The one by th'other' (3.1.110–13). Coriolanus here offers perhaps the best testament against claims that he strives to stand apart from linguistic communities, for he asserts that language – and specifically ordered, governed language – is necessary to determine where one stands in the world. It is when agitators begin speaking out of turn – 'and such a one as he, who puts his "shall", / His popular "shall", against a graver bench' (3.1.106–107) – that chaos ensues. Particularly telling is that Coriolanus subtly conflates the social and personal implications of such bids for linguistic control. He first couches his disapproval in an argument for the retention of social distinction, so that senators and patricians may be prevented from being reduced to 'common fools'. For this reason, the 'popular shall' – quite literally, the *shall* of the people – is an oxymoron to Coriolanus; it is not only threatening, but untenable, for the language of the people cannot reduplicate that of the patricians. The result of such laxity, according to Coriolanus, is a dangerous linguistic intermingling, wherein 'when, both your voices blended, the great'st taste / Most palates theirs' (3.1.104–105); in other words, the resulting blended voice will always favour the people. Coriolanus's fixed opinions on the need for effective leadership are evident, but this general political ideology is necessarily bound up with an awareness of what is at stake for Coriolanus personally, so that collective concerns, such as fear of tainted language, bleed into fears about individual self-protection. The speech begins with the tone of an outraged but still distanced orator; the subject is the derided 'he', the audience the collective 'you', and Coriolanus's own 'I' perspective is withheld.

Yet this impersonal mask begins to crack as the speech continues; after appealing to 'Jove himself' (3.1.108), aligning himself with a difficult-to-topple authority, Coriolanus refers for the first time to his own pained state: 'My soul aches' (3.1.109). Further, as Cominius and Menenius attempt to halt his increasingly inflammatory rant and shunt him away – 'Well, on to th'market place' (3.1.113) – the more of himself Coriolanus injects into his comments. When Menenius urges, 'Well, well, no more of that' (3.1.117), Coriolanus (ever in the guise of linguistic controller), proceeds as if his ally had not spoken with a strong proclamation of his own: 'Though there the people had more absolute power – / I say they nourished disobedience' (3.1.118–19); he follows up with the equally assertive intention that 'I'll give my reasons, / More worthier than their voices' (3.1.120–1). The increasing frequency of personal pronouns suggests a burgeoning awareness of the implications of the citizens' seditious behaviour not only for the community at large, but for Coriolanus himself. More subtly, however, this self-reference represents a strategy for asserting control over the exchange. Just as Coriolanus, in refusing to address Sicinius, is capable of withholding the power of a conferred name, he is able to acknowledge and reinforce his own subject position by naming himself. By positioning himself as a real force, an *I* that cannot be disregarded, Coriolanus accelerates the conflict and renders it explicitly personal: the situation is transformed to him versus them, and he pits himself against precisely what they strive to expropriate (the 'absolute power' of their 'voices'). Coriolanus's retort reveals itself as a personal battle, and his defensive stance is a means of protecting his most valued attribute: his understanding of his own place in the world. Identity is shaped by the very conditions on which Coriolanus comments: who may speak, and from what context and perspective. The act of speaking is inextricably bound up with one's stance in the world: 'To speak is inevitably to situate one's self in the world, to take up a position, to engage with others in a process of production and exchange, to occupy a social space' (Hanks, 'Notes on Semantics' 139). Grammatical modality is one prominent means by which such a space is negotiated. In this case, Coriolanus envisions himself one way, but is not permitted to realize this vision; the position that he attempts to claim is denied.

Not only is Coriolanus forced to relinquish his customary modes of self-positioning, he must also relent to a new version of the future, renegotiated by others. Evidence for this reframed future is apparent as Coriolanus's rant is brought to an end, not by the pleas of his cohort but rather by the pithy and brutal directive of the tribunes:

BRUTUS
He's said enough.

SICINIUS
He's spoken like a traitor, and shall answer
As traitors do.

(3.1.163–5)

With these words, the tribunes lay down irrefutable proof of their power. Brutus's terminating words are definitively peremptory, putting a decisive end to the possibility of speech, while Sicinius's vow that he 'shall answer' acts as the trump card. This *shall*, hardly as impotent as Coriolanus had initially tried to categorize it, is confirmation that they have won, for it represents the 'absolute shall' that has changed hands from one set of rule-makers to another. Recall that the first verbal conflict in the scene occurs when the tribunes demand that Coriolanus and his party 'stop', even as the senators insist 'Tribunes, give way; he *shall* to th' market-place' (3.1.32; emphasis added). Sicinius's *shall* at the end of the scene confirms how the dispute over Coriolanus's immediate future is ultimately resolved, for it is the tribunes' version of the future that will be carried out. Coriolanus shall not go to the marketplace; he shall be punished as a traitor. Not only has he been publicly defeated in a verbal sparring match, he has also lost authority over all parties, including himself. It is only after Brutus and Sicinius utter these final condemning words that Coriolanus finally addresses his prosecutors, in the taunting, defensive language appropriate to the angry prisoner that he now is: 'Thou wretch, despite o'erwhelm thee!'; 'Hence, old goat' (3.1.164, 178). The progression that we have witnessed over the course of this scene – a trajectory beginning with Coriolanus's incredulous protests and ending with his forced passivity – unveils the machinations behind his self-appraisal and self-positioning. At the end of the 'absolute shall' scene, we are witness to the aftermath of a renegotiated subject who is forced to acknowledge the reversal of authority and a marked shift in the social space he is permitted to occupy.

The change in speech tendencies is not restricted to Coriolanus; consider the new momentum that the word *shall* acquires for those who have been pitted against Coriolanus up to this point. In the aftermath of the 'absolute shall' conflict, the tribunes and the citizens begin to use the word with abandon. *Shall* has been held up by Coriolanus as a powerful word that designates control, a word worth sparring over so that its winner may wield it like a prize. Having publicly won the right to claim 'absolute shall', the tribunes treat the word as a taboo profanity that they repeat with relish. It carries the intoxicating weight of something formerly inaccessible, but newly discovered to be within their grasp.

MENENIUS
  You worthy tribunes –

SICINIUS
  He shall be thrown down the Tarpeian rock
  With rigorous hands. He hath resisted law,
  And therefore law shall scorn him further trial
  Than the severity of the public power,
  Which he so sets at naught.

FIRST CITIZEN
  He shall well know
  The noble tribunes are the people's mouths,
  And we their hands.

ALL PLEBEIANS
  He shall, sure on't.

(3.1.268–74)

Sicinius seems to take particular delight in interrupting Menenius's feeble plea with his new injunction. The references to 'scorn' and 'the people's mouths' uphold the focus on the power and legitimacy of speech, and underscore the fact that the tribunes have won a decisive victory in this contested realm. Even the rhythm of the lines emphasizes the word; the repeated 'law' holds semantic properties that recall *shall*, and the lines 'He shall well know' and 'He shall, sure on it' carry alliterative force. In subsequent scenes, the new currency bestowed on *shall* ensures that the word imparts a weightier blow when it is used against Coriolanus. Indeed, it becomes a byword of sorts in Sicinius's proceedings against him; in his plotting with Brutus, Sicinius isolates *shall* as a literal call to arms: 'Assemble presently the people hither, / And when they hear me say "It shall be so" / I'th'right and strength o'th'commons', be it either / For death, for fine, or banishment, then let them, / If I say "Fine", cry "Fine!", if "Death", cry "Death!"' (3.3.13–17). True to his word, in his hortatory address to the citizens, Sicinius transforms this modal phrase into a rallying cry: 'I'th' people's name / I say it shall be so' (3.3.111–12); 'There's no more to be said, but he is banished / As enemy to the people and his country. / It shall be so' (3.3.124–6). The plebeians' response to the jingoism is fervent, even ecstatic: 'It shall be so, it shall be so! Let him away! / He's banished, and it shall be so!' (3.3.113–14). The desperate mob of the play's opening scene has come a long way; newly articulate, capable of backing their words with achieved power, they are in a sense answering their earlier call to 'speak, speak'.[11] In claiming this victory for the 'right and strength o'th'commons', the citizens highlight a feature of shared language: resources are limited, and so they must be fought for. In declaring that 'it shall be so', the plebeians claim the assurance that their words can felicitously determine a future event. This relationship between lawful access to language and actual power is not lost on Brutus, who boasts, 'Now we have shown our power' (4.2.3).

The confrontation between Coriolanus and the tribunes exemplifies Coriolanus's preferred method of expressing convictions about himself and the state of his world: not through the self-reflective musings of soliloquy, but rather during the skirmishes in which he seems so at home. Dialogue provides a valuable store of information by showcasing the speaker in the process of self-positioning and negotiation, and the details of Coriolanus's verbal performance offer a revealing linguistic profile. Coriolanus's famous declaration as he is confronted with the pleas of his wife and mother – 'I'll never / Be such a gosling to obey instinct, but stand / As if a man were author of himself / And knew no other kin' (5.3.34–7) – is often cited as a decisive appeal to autonomy and detachment. Yet Coriolanus's desire to be 'author of himself' – as the one who originates, who causes an action or event to come into being – perhaps speaks less to a desire for severed bonds than to a wish for control over uncertain future events. It is, in a sense, a wish to return to his acknowledged role as 'god to punish' rather than man 'of infirmity', capable of falling prey to instinct. Aware that language is built on exchange, Coriolanus maintains a goal of mastery in linguistic encounters; he relishes these reciprocal situations when they allow him to affirm his dominance. This is why the 'absolute shall' scene represents such a resounding loss. By aggressively challenging the impinging *shalls* of the tribunes, Coriolanus discloses his alarm of being outstripped as the regulator of discourse. And as the repercussions of the 'absolute shall' scene show, words to which Coriolanus feels exclusively entitled are ultimately turned against him, and he is stripped of his capacity to speak a powerful future-determining word.

Part of Coriolanus's ultimate defeat, then, is the reversal of his wished-for status as 'author' of himself and his future by the end of the play. Allied with Aufidius, estranged from the city and his family, Coriolanus appears to face down the approach of his mother and wife with typical steeliness: 'Shall I be tempted to infringe my vow / In the same time 'tis made? I will not' (5.3.20–1). Yet the progression of his modals is telling; in the shift from the *shall* to *will*, Coriolanus slides the emphasis from resolute obligation to the more vulnerable area of personal volition, and thus foreshadows the capitulation to which he is about to yield. Coriolanus's words, while putatively addressed to Aufidius, sound more like a soliloquy, a plaintive bargain with the universe. But in launching his 'will' so nakedly into the world, Coriolanus places himself on shaky ground; as the play has consistently demonstrated, the world is no safe place for ephemeral individual will. It will be caught up and assimilated by various competing wills, particularly those with the powerful tug of maternal propriety. Volumnia has altered Coriolanus's will in the past, and his statement covertly suggests his recognition that she can do it again. Even before she has spoken, his words begin to falter – 'I prate' (5.3.48).

True to form, Volumnia's manoeuver is masterful. She begins with uncharacteristically soft persuasion: 'Yet we will ask, / That, if you fail in our request, the blame / May hang upon your hardness. Therefore hear us' (5.3.89–91). Her statement carries a whiff of deference, but it is damning as well as damaging; the underhanded words place the initial emphasis on her own volition – 'we will ask' – but use the slippery 'may' to solicit his permission to blame himself. Coriolanus answers in a way reminiscent of his response to the tribunes in the 'absolute shall' scene, refusing to grant his persecutor the privilege of personal address: 'Aufidius and you Volsces, mark, for we'll / Hear nought from Rome in private' (5.3.92–3). Volumnia, undaunted, redirects the authority to herself:

> For myself, son,
> I purpose not to wait on fortune till
> These wars determine. If I cannot persuade thee
> Rather to show a noble grace to both parts
> Than seek the end of one, thou shalt no sooner
> March to assault thy country than to tread –
> Trust to't, thou shalt not – on thy mother's womb
> That brought thee to this world.
>
> (5.3.118–24)

Her emphatic repetition of the commandment-like 'thou shalt not' ensures that Coriolanus cannot mistake the meaning behind her words.[12] Here, Volumina deploys the authentic 'absolute shall' that she knows will vanquish her son. Her pronouncement shows remarkable effrontery in deploying a word that has so publicly victimized Coriolanus. After stripping Coriolanus of agency over his own future, Volumnia's final triumph comes as she, again, compels him to alter his own will to conform with her own: 'Say my request's unjust, / And spurn me back. But, if it be not so, / Thou art not honest' (5.3.164–6).

Coriolanus's moment of surrender in the wake of his mother's rhetorical manipulation features an unusual and poignant stage direction: *He holds her by the hand, silent.* Volumnia's words prove to be genuinely peremptory, finally severing any illusion of control through speech that Coriolanus may have retained up to this point. The tableau is a visual representation of Volumnia's resonant 'thou shalt not' commandment. Indeed, after this moment, the voluble Coriolanus is effectively silenced. He plaintively seeks Aufidius's approval – 'Now, good Aufidius, / Were you in my stead, would you have heard / A mother less? Or granted less, Aufidius?' (5.3.191–3) – and acknowledges his renegotiated future: 'I'll not to Rome; I'll back with you' (5.3.198). Upon his prescribed return to Rome, Coriolanus relies on impotent threats in his confrontation with Aufidius. Coriolanus's last articulation of the future, dictated for Aufidius, is in fact the fate that he himself suffers in short order: 'Your judgements, my grave lords, / Must give this cur the lie; and his own notion – / Who wears my stripes impressed upon him, that / Must bear my beating to his grave – shall join / To thrust the lie unto him' (5.6.107–11).

Aufidius's eulogizing words, after Coriolanus is killed, are provisional and tinged with irony: 'Though in this city he / Hath widowed and unchilded many a one, / Which to this hour bewail the injury, / Yet he shall have a noble memory' (5.6.152–5). Aufidius here emphasizes the voices of others, the common people who 'bewail' the hurts inflicted by Coriolanus. Aufidius's tribute to them is a final confirmation of the injunction spoken by Sicinius, which seems to act as a motto for the play: 'Sir, the people / Must have their voices' (2.2.135–6). The last *shall* of the play marks a future determined by Aufidius, and it too is vaguely damning. 'Yet he shall have a noble memory' recalls one of the sarcastic insults directed by Menenius to the tribunes: 'A pair of tribunes that have wracked for Rome / To make coals cheap – a noble memory!' (5.1.16–17). That it is reiterated here undermines any promise for Coriolanus's legacy: he is not the sacrificial victim whose vision will live on, but rather the dupe whose enemies have succeeded in turning the tables. The parameters of Coriolanus's battle to speak his place in the world, and the details of the loss of this fight, are inscribed in the telling words of the 'absolute shall' scene and the final moment of capitulation. The words that Coriolanus fights for with such ferocity are held up as keys to interactional control. Unlike Volumnia's 'Trust to't, thou shalt not', Coriolanus's words are ultimately binding to no one, and to no future. It is this utter impotence, so publicly bestowed, that is a source of tragic experience – it is less noble sacrifice and more the thwarting of a would-be leader whose adversaries are always granted the last word that he so covets.

2

Troilus and Cressida: 'Do you think I will?'

Idiosyncratic and difficult to categorize, *Troilus and Cressida* can come off rather like a dramatic experiment. Its stylistic and linguistic curiosities demand vigilant attention from its audience, who must move uneasily among petty quarrels, lofty disquisitions and bawdy gossip. *Troilus and Cressida*'s history of performance, reception and interpretation is also vexed by questions of language. The play is a piecemeal work, binding elements of popular drama, genteel debate and epic poetry (itself filtered through a well-established English tradition).[1] Given the collision of these genres and influences, it is not surprising that the play has been seen as linguistically incongruous and excessive. *Troilus and Cressida* tests the limits of its medium, defying the expectations of its audience and seeming to retreat from conventional storytelling modes in order to use the conditions of performance to explore social ideas and types. With its many scenes of public debate and its tendency towards overwrought dialogue, *Troilus and Cressida* turns a spotlight on moments of linguistic fracture, tension and disjointedness. Speakers in *Troilus and Cressida* are disillusioned not only with their circumstances and with each other, but also with language itself, the primary interface by means of which they interact with their world.

This peculiar play offers a rich case study for audiences and scholars with an interest in language. Its range of varied and unsettling dialogue renders it an ideal text in which to explore the details of linguistic exchange. This chapter uses the framework of discourse analysis to consider the language of *Troilus and Cressida*. In its loosest definition, discourse analysis is 'the analysis of language-in-use whether spoken or written' (Gee 205). Unlike some other forms of linguistic analysis – or, in traditional literary scholarship, close reading – discourse analysis is concerned primarily with the dialogic and the social aspects of language-in-use; it is *conversation* – the meanings, effects and negotiations of spoken dialogue – that is made central in this method. Such an approach has much to offer scholars of Shakespeare, because the bulk of our primary material is dialogue – dramatic dialogue rather than 'actual' dialogue, to be sure, but adherent nevertheless to the rules and patterns of naturally occurring speech. Discourse analysis equips critics with tools for thinking about the underpinnings, motivations and artful deployment of speech, and specifically the 'socially situated' linguistic exchanges that are fundamental to dramatic discourse (Magnusson, *Shakespeare and Social Dialogue* 1).

Over the past several decades, discourse analysis has been sporadically integrated into Shakespeare criticism, with varying degrees of impact and success. Typically, these sorts of analyses apply tools gleaned from the study of naturally occurring dialogue and conversation to dramatic discourse. Features held up for analysis include turn-taking among speakers, linguistically embedded signals of social power and status, such as terms of address, and the types of utterances produced by speakers (directives, challenges, questions and so on). More broadly, discourse analysis queries the ways that context, social and cultural influences, and power structures inform the discourse, both subtly and overtly. In a pioneering essay, 'Changing the Guard at Elsinore' (1989), Walter Nash breaks down the familiar opening of *Hamlet* – beyond the perennially intriguing 'Who's there?' – using standard techniques of discourse analysis. First, he offers a paraphrase of the conversation between Bernardo and Francisco, an exercise that (as he admits) 'reduce[s] to modern banality the sharp impact of Shakespeare's dramatic language'. At the same time, it focuses attention on the mechanics of interaction and exchange, inviting a 'direct reading of motives' (24). Nash suggests that paraphrase is 'not simply a translation of the scene into modern colloquial English, but also an interpretation, or more precisely a close series of interpretations, from sentence to sentence, emphasis to emphasis, inflection to inflection' (24). Nash's explanation emphasizes the scene as dialogue rather than simply as literary language; in the paraphrase, we become aware of the motives that underlie each spoken word. This approach encourages us to read the words as *utterances*, as language-in-conversation that is socially motivated and informed by the concerns and pressures of spoken interaction. This provides an apt starting point for a close, line-by-line commentary and analysis in which Nash traces the 'transaction structure' of the dialogue:

> The first task of the discourse analyst describing patterns of conversation is to determine their structure as a complex of exchanges minimally represented as I(nitiation) and R(esponse) ... the IR structure is related to a hierarchy in which the comprehensive unit is the *interaction*, comprising *transactions* between certain speakers on certain topics, realized in *exchanges* governing the phasing of the topic, the exchanges being worked out in *moves*, for example, opening moves, supporting moves, challenging moves, expounded by specific verbal *acts*, of eliciting, directing, informing, commenting, acknowledging and so forth. (22; emphasis in original)

By examining the 'moves' of the first twenty-nine lines of *Hamlet*, Nash's analysis throws into relief elements such as the structure of the discourse (who is asking questions? who is initiating 'moves'?), 'implicatures' (the impulses and meanings behind the usage of certain words and types of phrases), and situational power and 'face' (the double-edged desire to be approved of and also to be free from the imposition of others in interaction).[2] In *Hamlet*, Nash concludes, there is a subtle yet compelling early emphasis on Bernardo's authority. In this case, discourse analysis prompts us to take a close look at the characterization of Bernardo as Shakespeare initiates us into the world of the play. Nash claims that 'Bernardo's brief role is a curious one, and subtler than we may at first be disposed to think' (38). The anxieties, questions and withheld information revealed by an analysis of Bernardo's conversational role suggest that this 'very minor character' is improbably significant and even 'indispensable' (40). Nash is careful to maintain that the impression of Bernardo's importance can be gleaned from a more general reading, one that is less focused on the details of dialogue. The benefits of discourse analysis, in Nash's view, are the unveiling of the workings behind 'common sense intuitions'; discourse analysis can confirm, 'with additional emphasis and a sharpening of focus', the impressions of a more casual sort of reading (40).

Thirty years after its publication, 'Changing the Guard at Elsinore' stands as a testament to both the virtues and pitfalls of applying discourse analysis to Shakespeare's language. On the one hand, the method encourages an exposition of *how* meaning is made. Intuitive or 'common sense' readings are stripped down to their discursive elements, in a way that challenges notions of linguistic transparency too often taken for granted in literary criticism. On the other hand, jargon such as 'IR structure', and the labelling of talk as 'transactions between speakers', is bound to raise the eyebrows of critics trained in literary studies – the reduction of complex questions of aesthetics to crude formulas violates an essential, and sound, tenet of humanities research. The vaguely scientific terminology (and often too-stark conclusions) of literary discourse analysis has doubtless contributed to the reluctance of literary scholars to embrace it. Still, one prominent benefit of Nash's methodology is the frank attention it pays to the building blocks of communication. His work shows how discourse analysis can expose the mechanics of language use – the seams and tendencies – that inform our implicit assumptions about a literary text. It thus offers a means of supporting intuitive impressions, while at the same time it provides a window into perspectives that are easily overlooked. Nash's argument for the relative significance of Bernardo's character highlights both these advantages. As literary critics, we are trained to treat narrative beginnings with special attention; we recognize that it is significant that *Hamlet* opens with a question, just as we discern an aura of unease from the details of the setting (dark, cold, isolated). The methodology of discourse analysis extends the roots of unease to the patterns of dialogue demonstrated by Bernardo, and it further suggests that Bernardo's character is not simply a placeholder.

Just as discourse analysis has been used to support implicit assumptions and trace the mechanics of meaning-making in Shakespeare's works, it has also been employed to challenge prevailing assumptions. In a 1994 essay, Clara Calvo argues that, while the bulk of critical attention has been paid to *As You Like It*'s eloquent Rosalind, the comparatively retiring Celia is due for some consideration. The essay presents a case in which an intuitive understanding – that Rosalind is the play's most accomplished speaker – is tested by the methods of discourse analysis. Calvo traces discourse strategies such as turn-taking and discourse initiation to show that Celia's character takes control of far more of the dialogue than she tends to be given credit for. As Calvo explains, Celia's character has mastered the precepts of conversational turn-taking, and recognizes how to use them to her advantage: 'the right to enjoy an extended conversational turn [and] the right not to be interrupted while she delivers the information Rosalind has requested of her' (105). The structure of the play's dialogue, and the way that speakers understand and manipulate the conventions of talk, become under this approach a fertile arena for analysis and interpretation. Like Nash's essay, however, Calvo's features many instances of terminology imported wholesale from discourse studies, and literary scholars may recoil from terms like 'feedback moves' and 'transaction relevance places'.

Some of the most comprehensive and productive readings of Shakespeare's work using the techniques of discourse analysis emerge from Magnusson's *Shakespeare and Social Dialogue: Dramatic Language and Elizabethan Letters* (1999). Magnusson uses tools borrowed from discourse analysis to analyse the fundamentally social nature of Shakespeare's language and to expose the ways that language is 'organized as interaction, how dialogue and other verbal exchanges can be shaped by the social scene or context as much as individual speakers' (1). Magnusson takes the important step of adapting a discourse-based methodology for literary critics; she argues that discourse analysis, with its 'accent on dialogic interaction and on the situated use of language in its varied contexts' equips critics with tools for thinking about the underpinnings, motivations and artful deployment of speech, and specifically the 'types of socially situated verbal exchange[s]' that are central to a dramatist's art (2). By borrowing tools from a specialized area of linguistics and mapping them onto the study of dramatic dialogue, and retaining a literary critic's attunement to the aesthetic ends of literary representations of speech, Magnusson demonstrates how recent innovative work in language-related fields can revive and illuminate areas that have stagnated in literary studies.

As the brief examples described above suggest, a prominent benefit of discourse analysis is its capacity to trace the roots of impressionistic reading. It encourages consideration of the dialogic workings of a text, bringing the mechanics of meaning-making into sharper focus. Whereas literary criticism generally directs attention to questions of signification and representation, discourse analysis 'focuses on how this significance can be related to specific features of language, to the linguistic texture of a literary text' (Verdonk 55). Of course, such directed attention is the purview of all forms of close reading, to some extent. To perform a close reading is to link a work's formal and linguistic features to characterization, theme and – to invoke the guiding principle of the New Critics, for whom close reading was paramount – 'unity' or cohesion of the work. Perhaps its overlap with outmoded formalist approaches is one of the most pointed strikes against discourse analysis. Discourse analysis may understandably be seen as dressing old methods in a modish new lexicon; it might also be viewed as regression to a time in which details of context, culture and history were jettisoned in favour of vague aesthetic judgements. Yet the elements that distinguish discourse analysis from formalist precursors are those that may salvage it from these types of critiques: it is fundamentally context-bound, by definition taking its precepts from the social dimensions of linguistic interaction.

Also of critical concern is the fact that the methodology of discourse analysis is rarely historicized. It's one thing to apply discourse analysis to the dramatic dialogue of contemporary dramatic works; because they largely adhere to the conventions of style, syntax and grammar of present-day English, modern plays readily align with the methods of discourse analysis. It's quite another matter to use discourse analysis to illuminate the language of a work such as *The Tempest*. To take one example, the act of using an imperative in dialogue tends to be marked in discourse analysis; it is indicative of a speaker who is exercising power or making a bid for control. Yet while imperatives are relatively uncommon in present-day English (found in an average of one in ten requests), in early modern English they were less remarkable (evident in an average of one in three requests) (Culpeper and Archer 61). We can conclude, then, that an early modern English speaker's use of an imperative does not always have the associations of force or impingement of will that it does today. Prospero's 'Hag seed, hence!' (*Tem* 1.2.367) signals authoritative control in a way that 'let be' (*Ham* 5.2.201) does not. In cases such as these, strict adherence to the findings of discourse analysis will lead to a misleading, or at least incomplete, reading of the underpinnings of Shakespeare's dialogue.

Why, then, might we use a form of analysis that encourages attention to the ways that meanings are made and effects enacted in language when such practices are already arguably at the heart of literary study? How are these methods different from other tools of close reading? As the example from Walter Nash illustrates, it is not always the case that the discourse analysis will unveil something entirely novel and unexpected to readers and audiences; however, what it helps to expose is the practices and strategies that inform our implicit understandings. Discourse analysis exposes the underpinnings of what we think of as natural responses. It's a means of supporting intuitive impressions, and it can also give us a glimpse into perspectives that are easily overlooked. In a play like *Troilus and Cressida*, where dialogic interaction is particularly fraught and overdetermined, discourse analysis helps to bring to light the foundations of its conflicts.

In *Troilus and Cressida*'s stalemated Troy, love affairs are matters of public debate and grounds for war, and the influence of meddlesome relatives and disgruntled comrades is inescapable. The play has been a touchstone for critics interested in identity, who have identified the ways in which characters in the play fruitlessly seek to create or recreate themselves and one another.[3] *Troilus and Cressida*'s insistence that identity itself is dependent on others is captured in Achilles' famous words on reciprocal observation and appraisal: 'nor doth the eye itself, / That most pure spirit of sense, behold itself, / Not going from itself, but eye to eye opposed, / Salutes each other with each other's form, / For speculation turns not to itself / Till it hath traveled and is mirrored there / Where it may see itself' (3.3.105–12). A subject cannot see himself, cannot *be* himself, except in interaction with another. This collaborative inevitability may be seen as a necessary condition of being human, but the suggestion in *Troilus and Cressida* is that all interaction is mired in suspicion. Ulysses clearly voices these anxieties in his familiar hierarchy speech – 'O, when degree is shaked, / Which is the ladder of all high designs, / The enterprise is sick' (1.3.101–103) – and in his incisive recognition that worth is derived from without, in the perceptions of other people: 'no man is the lord of anything, / Though in and of him there be much consisting, / Till he communicate his parts to others' (3.3.116–18). The conviction that value is realized only when it is affirmed by others reflects a widespread mistrust of dependence, and an accompanying cynicism about human communication.

From its opening scene, *Troilus and Cressida* holds up to scrutiny the effects of shared language, and even the most banal conversations show speakers attempting to harness words to serve their own meanings and their own intentions. The insouciance of the Prologue, who proclaims his indifference to his audience by suggesting that their reactions are of little consequence – 'Like or find fault; do as your pleasures are' (30) – is quickly replaced with a tenor of competition in the talk between Troilus and Pandarus that opens the first act. This initial linguistic encounter, while amusing in its disclosure of character – Troilus's single-minded lovesickness countered by Pandarus's obstinate refusal to empathize – shows each speaker striving to make claims on specific words, corralling his interlocutor to speak according to the conditions determined by him. Pandarus's mock vow to 'meddle nor make no further' is followed by a pronouncement bound to provoke Troilus into a prescribed response: 'He that will have a cake out of the wheat must tarry the grinding' (1.1.14–15). Troilus, rising to the bait, meets each of Pandarus's retorts with the same answer in a relentless attempt to wrench agreement from him:

TROILUS
Have I not tarried?

PANDARUS
Ay, the grinding; but you must tarry the bolting.

TROILUS
Have I not tarried?

PANDARUS
Ay, the bolting; but you must tarry the leavening.

TROILUS
Still have I tarried.

PANDARUS
>Ay, to the leavening; but here's yet in the word hereafter the kneading, the making of the cake, the heating the oven, and the baking. Nay, you must stay the cooling too, or ye may chance burn your lips.

>(1.3.16–24)

This comic exchange establishes conversational tendencies that will be carried throughout the play; bickering is a favoured means of communication, and any conversation that veers towards earnest emotion will be swiftly undercut by satire or mockery. In the face of Pandarus's unwillingness to provide the answer that he seeks, Troilus provides it for himself – 'Still I have tarried' – while the undaunted Pandarus persists with his own thread of conversation, even recanting the conditional 'Ay's he has conceded with a final dismissive 'nay'.

An approach rooted in discourse analysis helps to illuminate the conversational details that underlie each speaker's motivations and strategies in this exchange. H.P. Grice's theory of conversational implicature, a foundational tool of discourse analysis, posits a series of maxims that provide a template for the exchange of information in dialogue. These maxims include quality (saying what you believe to be true); quantity (giving the right amount of information); relation (being relevant); and manner (being clear).[4] Grice understood discourse as fundamentally collaborative, a 'joint project in which the interlocutors aim at achieving one or more common goals' (Geurts 10). Here, Pandarus fails – albeit playfully – to obey a basic tenet of conversation: 'make your conversational contribution such as is required, at the stage at which it occurs, by the accepted purpose or direction of the talk exchange in which you are engaged' (Grice 26). In Gricean terms, the 'co-operative principle' by which speakers contribute according to the accepted purpose or direction of the talk exchange is violated.

In one sense, the exchange between Pandarus and Troilus shows how conversations can be competitive operations, as each speaker vies for a measure of control: 'By taking the discourse further, by initiating new topical aspects, he or she tries to govern the contributions to follow. Hence, there is a basic asymmetry involved in this dialectic between being controlled and being in control, which is part and parcel of the "power" of basic dialogue mechanisms' (Linell and Luckmann 7). In this case, though, the competitive nature of the interaction is exaggerated; Troilus and Pandarus each attempt not only to govern the response of his addressee, but in fact strive to dictate it. As Pandarus continues to goad Troilus with his appraisal of Cressida – 'An her hair were not somewhat darker than Helen's' (39) – Troilus calls on the rules of cooperative conversation and accuses Pandarus of playing false: 'I tell thee, Pandarus, / When I do tell thee there my hopes lie drowned, / Reply not in how many fathoms deep / They lie indrenched. I tell thee I am mad / In Cressid's love, thou answer'st "She is fair"' (45–9). Yet this protest, too, illustrates the problem of cooperation. Despite his attempts to instruct, Troilus cannot prescribe how Pandarus will 'reply'. The conundrum – that the rules and substance of dialogue must be mutually negotiated – is neatly expressed a few lines later:

PANDARUS
I speak no more than truth.

TROILUS
Thou dost not speak so much.

(61–2)

The disagreed-upon substance of 'truth,' the stuff of dialogue that these speakers share, represents the differences between them, and the dangers to which they are subjected in the realm of speech.[5] Troilus's complaint about the slipperiness of words – 'Words, words, mere words, no matter from the heart; / Th'effect doth operate another way' (5.3.107–108) – succinctly captures this problem. Linguistic meaning is the sum of many parts, with 'mouth' and 'heart' only two of many contributors at work in the production of meaning. The 'network of assumptions and inferences permeating even the simplest of conversations' (Werth 9) is laid bare in the exchange above, as Pandarus exploits several factors – including his understanding of Troilus's lovesickness and their shared community in which Helen is a potent symbol – in order to provoke Troilus. In this instance, Pandarus adopts a teasing role, breaking unspoken 'rules' of conversation to pester the unwitting Troilus. Yet this early dialogue suggests that simply parsing the words that are uttered will not produce a nuanced understanding of talk, and this awareness resonates throughout the play.

As the scene between Troilus and Pandarus lightheartedly demonstrates, competition is a key component of the network of voices in *Troilus and Cressida*. In this dramatic word, there is no shortage of characters vying for the position of dominant speaker. Thersites is the resident commentator who invariably punctures the lofty pronouncements of those whom he observes, Ulysses the shrewd rhetorician, and Troilus the self-assured young upstart. It is no accident that theses claimants to linguistic mastery are invariably male, spokesmen for a martial world whose conditions stem from a competition over a woman. The play consistently, and conspicuously, points to the silencing of female characters. Hector responds to Andromache's concerns about his imminent battle by dismissing her as a nag and demanding her departure: 'I am offended with you. / Upon the love you bear me, get you in' (5.3.77–8). Troilus similarly scorns Cassandra as a 'foolish, dreaming, superstitious girl' (5.3.79). The fears of these disdained female characters are ultimately borne out, but the women of *Troilus and Cressida* are relegated to the margins of the primary action, pawns and bystanders in the world of men.

The character of Cressida seems particularly ensnared in a predetermined identity. In the words of the play's acid-tongued critic, Thersites, Cressida is a 'Trojan drab' (5.1.94) apparently destined to fulfil her fate as the quintessentially false woman. The critical reception of Cressida's character has tended to hew closely to this observation; Cressida's betrayal is ordained by her prominent cultural legacy, and she is fated to behave the way she does. In this sense, she becomes less a fully realized character than a symbol in an offbeat play. When *Troilus and Cressida* begins, audiences are granted close access to a witty and inventive speaker. Cressida, initially, is a sharp interlocutor, full of playful quips and bawdy rejoinders. By the end of the play, though, her voice is markedly silent. We witness her transformed from one of the play's most compelling and authoritative speakers into a vanished voice, whose words are reduced to fragments.

Cressida's character would appear at first glance to fit the pattern of the play's other female speakers. Her voice goes largely unheeded, particularly when she protests her trade to the Greek camp. Her final silencing is the most potent and visually striking in the play; shrouded in a letter to Troilus, her words are physically fragmented as he tears them up, unread. In a play so concerned with clashing wills, and debates about individual desire versus the collective good, Cressida's indications of volition and desire tend to be overlooked, perhaps because she is so decisively obscured by the end of the play. Yet Cressida's dialogue offers a practical example of the benefits of discourse analysis. When we test out the methods of discourse analysis and pay attention to the nuances of Cressida's speech – and the ways in which her powerful will is exerted and then thwarted – we can find bids for agency and dominance that align her with the play's other vying speakers.

In the play's opening scene, Cressida is introduced indirectly when Troilus laments that he is 'mad / In Cressid's love' (1.1.48–9) and begs Pandarus to intervene on his love sick behalf. His plea includes a blazon worthy of the most ardent sonneteer:

> Her eyes, her hair, her cheek, her gait, her voice;
> Handlest in thy discourse, O, that her hand,
> In whose comparison all whites are ink
> Writing their own reproach; to whose soft seizure
> The cygnet's down is harsh, and spirit of sense
> Hard as the palm of ploughmen.
>
> (1.1.51–6)

The audience's first impression of Cressida is doubly familiar. Her name itself is a giveaway, shackling her to a 'notorious identity' as an infamously false lover.[6] In Troilus's depiction, she is an abstract ideal, a love object akin to those in countless Elizabethan lyrics. Her predecessors in Shakespeare's canon – which include the addressees in the sonnets and Romeo's Rosaline – are typically voiceless figures in their respective texts. Troilus's courtly language continues on its predictable hyperbolic track as he imagines her as a rare spoil to be acquired through brokerage and risky feats:

> Her bed is India; there she lies, a pearl.
> Between our Ilium and where she resides,
> Let it be called the wild and wand'ring flood,
> Ourself the merchant, and this sailing Pandar
> Our doubtful hope, our convoy and our bark.
>
> (1.1.96–100)

This characterization recalls Tarquin's reflections as he approaches the sleeping Lucrece: 'Pain pays the income of each precious thing: / Huge rocks, high winds, strong pirates, shelves, and sands / The merchant fears ere rich at home he lands' (*Luc* 334–6). The acquisition of the love object is made sweeter, and more thrilling, by the obstacles that stand between the lover and his goal. While readers eventually hear Lucrece speak, at this point in the poem she is asleep and unaware, a silent object upon whom such proprietary claims may be projected. The long tradition of courtly love conventions, of which Lucrece is part, ensures that audiences contending with Troilus's description of Cressida are well schooled in the rhetoric that he deploys. A certain expectation is created, and the picture of Cressida that is established in the play's first scene only serves to heighten curiosity about her character when she at last appears on stage.

The subversion and dismantling of stock character types and expectations in *Troilus and Cressida* is first demonstrated in the depiction of Cressida. The contrast between the projected

Cressida in the play's first scene – remote, silent and pure – and the embodied Cressida in the second – blunt, vocal and commanding – is amusingly stark. Cressida's is the first voice we hear in the play's second scene, and her words belie the impression created in the previous scene. Far from the abstract and aloof naïf that she appears in Troilus's assessment, Cressida proves to be a seasoned and nimble speaker. Always ready with a witty retort or pointed joke, Cressida is consistently given the first and last word in verbal exchanges:

CRESSIDA
  Who were those went by?

ALEXANDER
  Queen Hecuba and Helen.

CRESSIDA
  And whither go they?

ALEXANDER
  Up to the eastern tower,
  Whose height commands as subject all the vale,
  To see the battle. Hector, whose patience
  Is as a virtue fixed, today was moved ...

CRESSIDA
  What was his cause of anger?

(1.2.1–12)

Cressida's inquiries set her up as a curious and somewhat callow figure, an eager aspirant to the world of knowledge and gossip that surrounds her. It doesn't take a discourse analyst to recognize that Cressida asks a lot of questions, but the tools of discourse analysis help to understand the significance of her role as a questioner, and point to a subtle sort of control that contradicts her apparent naïveté. Because discourse analysis is rooted in the strategies of verbal exchange, it exposes the mechanics of the *why*, the motivations that underlie the choices speakers make.

In this case, the questions asked by Cressida are termed, in the lexicon of discourse analysis, '*wh*-interrogatives': questions used to elicit information, to establish the who, what, why, how, and so on. They are typical of speakers wishing to take 'an initiatory role' since they serve the various authoritative functions of interrogation, challenging prior talk, and achieving commands (Eggins and Slade 87). Moreover, repeated questions – those which make the speaker sound like an interrogator – are particularly controlling because they produce a pronounced one-sided sort of discourse (Herman, *Dramatic Discourse* 134).[7] Egalitarian dialogue features greater variety and reciprocity; both interlocutors will ask questions, and responses and interrogatives will be more evenly distributed. In the audience's first encounter with Cressida, she is represented as an inquisitive and engaged speaker, as well as a dominant one. Turn-taking, when speakers initiate or respond to speech, is a common tool in the kit of a discourse analyst, and Cressida is a champion turn-taker in this scene, consistently outpacing the 'turns' of others. However, context of communication is vital in discourse analysis, and one important caveat is that this verbal exchange features Cressida in dialogue with her servant, Alexander. It seems reasonable, given their social distance, that their conversation is skewed towards a dominant speaker; the authoritative dynamic is built in to the existing relationship between the participants.

Also noteworthy is that a reading grounded in discourse analysis places emphasis on the *types* rather than the frequency of utterances. Looking at the verbal exchange between Cressida and Alexander on the page, a clear division is evident. Because Cressida is the questioner and Alexander the supplicant respondent, his answers are significantly longer and more involved than her questions. Other types of close reading often value the number of lines spoken by a character (we often relate power with loquacity, citing the number of lines spoken by Shakespeare's characters as evidence of their status in the dramatic world and their importance to the play). This makes an intuitive kind of sense: more lines, more words and more stage time would appear to translate to greater significance and authority. Yet in some cases, brevity is power. In this scene, given the nature of Cressida's and Alexander's respective utterances (*wh*-interrogatives and responses), the opposite is true. Alexander speaks more because he must.

When Alexander is replaced by Pandarus as Cressida's conversation partner, the superficial balancing of the dialogue reflects the change in relationship. Pandarus is Cressida's uncle, not her servant, and so it is reasonable that she should cede some conversational space to him. Rather than the pattern of terse questions and extended answers that characterized the dialogue with Alexander, here the shape of the conversation resembles *stichomythia*, the rapid-fire turn-taking between interlocutors that customarily denotes heated discussion or witty exchange.[8] Cast in the language of discourse analysis, the turn-taking ratio between speakers becomes more balanced than it was in Cressida's prior interaction. Again, on the surface, such a shift suits the context; we see the power shift when Cressida moves from speaking from Alexander to Pandarus, and the content of their dialogue reflects a witty exchange rooted in gossip and innuendo. Yet if we consider the types of utterances spoken in this exchange, we see that the dominant speaker position is retained by Cressida throughout. Although Pandarus's responses are briefer than Alexander's, and although he is permitted rejoinders and questions denied to Alexander, he remains in a reactive rather than an initiatory role. The nature of Cressida's utterances here are fundamentally different from those of Pandarus, and they are characteristic of speakers with more relative power:

CRESSIDA
   He is not Hector.

PANDARUS
   Himself? No, he's not himself, would 'a were himself!
                                                    (1.2.73–5)

CRESSIDA

Troilus will stand to the proof, if you'll prove it so.

PANDARUS

Troilus? Why, he esteems her no more than I esteem an addle egg.

(1.2.124–7)

In these examples, Pandarus's 'questions' are reiterations of Cressida's words; he challenges her assertions, but he remains in a responsive role.

PANDARUS

No, Hector is not a better man than Troilus.

CRESSIDA

Excuse me. [direct challenge]

PANDARUS

He is elder.

CRESSIDA

Pardon me, pardon me. [direct challenge]

(1.2.77–80)[9]

PANDARUS

I cannot choose but laugh to think how she tickled his chin. Indeed, she has a marvellous white hand, I must needs confess –

CRESSIDA

Without the rack. [interruption]

PANDARUS

And she takes upon her to spy a white hair on his chin.

CRESSIDA

Alas, poor chin! Many a wart is richer. [challenge]

PANDARUS

But there was such laughing! Queen Hecuba laughed that her eyes ran o'er –

CRESSIDA
With millstones. [interruption]

(1.2.130–9)

CRESSIDA
At what was all this laughing?

PANDARUS
Marry, at the white hair that Helen spied on Troilus' chin.

CRESSIDA
What was his answer? [*wh*-interrogatives]

(1.2.144–51)

Viewed simply as text on a page, these exchanges resemble a balanced dialogue (or perhaps one where the upper hand skews towards Pandarus), yet the nature of the utterances suggests otherwise. Cressida, as in her exchanges with Alexander, is with Pandarus the initiator and arbiter of dialogue. She guides its direction and determines its parameters. Discourse analysts note that two of the fundamental markers of bids for power in dialogue are the claiming of turns and utterances marked as authoritative, and Cressida excels in both areas: she claims her turn, sometimes aggressively, through challenges and interruptions, while she maintains a pattern of commanding utterances.[10]

The surprising fact of Cressida's authoritative speech is as stark rebuttal to Troilus's initial description; at the same time, the witty dialogue between Cressida and Pandarus is deftly positioned in the second scene of the play. In the first scene, we witnessed another amusing dialogue between Troilus and Pandarus, and if we contrast Pandarus's role as a speaker in these respective exchanges, we see him in a much more authoritative role in this initial conversation.

PANDARUS
Because she's kin to me, therefore she's not so fair as Helen; an she were not kin to me, she would be as fair o' Friday as Helen is on Sunday. But what care I? ... 'Tis all one to me.

TROILUS
> Say I she is not fair?

PANDARUS
> I do not care whether you do or no. She's a fool to stay behind her father; let her to the Greeks, and so I'll tell her the next time I see her. For my part, I'll meddle nor make no more i'th'matter.

TROILUS
> Pandarus –

PANDARUS
> Not I.

TROILUS
> Sweet Pandarus –

PANDARUS
> Pray you, speak no more to me; I will leave all as I found it. And there an end. [*Exit*]

(1.1.71–88)

Here, Pandarus dramatically interrupts, commands and contradicts. He determines the boundaries of the dialogue by categorically closing it. It is striking that in these back-to-back scenes initiating us into the world of the play, the speaker who is granted the most weight is Cressida. She is the sole speaker invariably in control of her dialogic exchanges. Later in the play, she confesses that she wishes herself a man, 'or that we women had men's privilege / Of speaking first' (3.2.124–5), yet in this early scene we witness her claiming that privilege.

Cressida's dialogue early in the play complicates some popular assumptions about her character. Rather than merely inhabiting a prescribed role, her characterization pushes against expectations from the outset. In the first act, she recalls Shakespeare's witty and commanding female speakers such as Beatrice and Cleopatra. Yet, early on, Cressida identifies her speech as an imperiling liability. In taking the male liberty of speaking first, she worries that she is betraying too much – 'for in this rapture I shall surely speak / The thing I shall repent ... Stop my mouth' (3.2.126–7, 129). Even in this mode of self-doubt, itself perhaps intended to lull Troilus into a reciprocal frankness, Cressida is clear-eyed about the ways that a speaker can attempt to control the responses of her interlocutor: 'Perchance, my lord, I show more craft than love / And fell so roundly to a large confession / To angle for your thoughts' (3.2.148–50). In other words, she discloses in order to receive confidences in turn. Of course, Cressida's confident speech, and her nuanced understanding of its unspoken parameters, is often aligned with her perceived sexual availability. Her skilful conversational tactics extend to the scene where she banters self-assuredly with the Greek soldiers, capably meeting their lusty inquiries with retorts and innuendo. Ulysses, in observing this 'woman of quick sense', as Nestor calls her (4.5.54), memorably aligns her words with her apparently vociferous body, and warns of her corrupting influence:

> Fie, fie upon her!
> There's language in her eye, her cheek, her lip,
> Nay, her foot speaks; her wanton spirits look out
> At every joint and motive of her body.
> O, these encounterers, so glib of tongue,
> That give accosting welcome ere it comes,
> And wide unclasp the tables of their thoughts
> To every ticklish reader! Set them down
> For sluttish spoils of opportunity
> And daughters of the game.
>
> (4.5.55–64)

Ulysses' characterization supports the idea that Cressida is the fulfilment of a pre-existing type, the false wanton, her open speech reflective of her fickle and unguarded sexual nature. His characterization of Cressida as an 'encounterer' – an unusual word with etymological roots in the adversarial *contra* – points transparently to her apparent appetite for sexual encounters, while at the same time it highlights the competitive arena of social language in which she excels. And while there are good reasons to be attuned to Cressida's 'glib' tongue, her harsh representation through the eyes of other characters is consistently undercut by her own appearances on stage. We in the audience are consistently directed to pay attention to ways in which Cressida defies expectation. Moreover, her tactics for self-assertion align her with Shakespeare's speakers with whom we are meant to sympathize. She is quick, playful and disarmingly frank in her speech. If we understand volition as a form of agency, the capacity to decide and to act, then Cressida's speech here inscribes this, for she is the one shaping the dialogue, making the decisions that determine its outcomes. An expectation is created, and then thwarted: Cressida the capable and authoritative interlocutor (in a play that has few) disappears incrementally as the play progresses. This is of particular significance in a play that so deliberately displaces action with talk; as Patricia Parker has suggested, *Troilus and Cressida*'s surplus of language ensures that its characters are defined through their speech (often at the expense of action), creating a milieu where 'words trump deeds' (221).

I have been considering broad patterns of discourse and control, including turn-taking and the types of utterances used by Cressida's character. Yet it is not only Cressida's early conversational successes that are worth noting; her lexical patterns are also telling. Certain words and collocations recur throughout the play and may be illuminated through the processes of discourse analysis, particularly using the methodology of the linguist M.A.K. Halliday. Halliday's theory of 'functional grammar' has been remarkably generative in the field of discourse analysis, highlighting the ways in which discourse works to signal unspoken meanings in addition to direct ones, while at the same time it retains a consistent focus on the context of the exchange. Halliday's model is premised on the idea that 'language is defined and shaped by the communicative functions it is used to perform' (Chapman 181), and it insists that pragmatic meaning is central to our understanding of language, beyond its grammar and structure.

It was one of the first and most influential models to explicitly link pragmatics to the study of grammar by tracing the meaning of a sentence 'to an illocutionary intention (and thus, the sentence itself to its utterance), as well as by indicating the special kind of relationship between the level of the sentence and that of the discourse/text and the communicative setting in which it is embedded' (Brisard 5). In other words, Halliday's approach recognizes that grammar, as we commonly understand it, is abstract and incomplete; we must always also take into account the ways in which interpersonal and spatial factors, alongside other contextual influences, inform and shape linguistic structure. Like all discourse analysts, Halliday understood language as both socially constitutive and socially determined. Unlike some, however, he was interested in the minutiae of discourse. Beyond discourse roles and utterance types, Halliday paid attention to lexical and grammatical elements of discourse, and showed how they functioned not simply as isolated elements within the discourse.[11] A key element of a Halliday-inflected approach to discourse analysis is attention to lexical cohesion, when a word is repeated at different points in the discourse. The repeated word acts as a signpost in the topography of the text that sets up a link between the various places where it occurs. It is cohesive because it offers a thread within the narrative, and its effect is not simply linear; it invokes a constellation of associations that move multidirectionally. It is a pattern in the system of the discourse. Other lexicogrammatical elements are also vital to a Hallidayan approach. In his landmark work *Linguistic Studies of Text and Discourse*, Halliday offers a detailed reading of Charles Darwin's *The Origin of the Species* that pairs a macro-level assessment of theme and motif in conjunction with a micro-level investigation of clauses, verbal groups and individual words. He argues for the singularly arresting use of 'evolved' in Darwin's final paragraph:

> Within the sentence, the word *evolved* has to carry a cumulative prominence ... it has to pick up the thematic

motif of explanation, and to secure total commitment to one explanation and rejection of the other ... Yet all this load of work is hardly worth mentioning beside the major responsibility the word *evolved* has to bear, along with the verbal group of which it is part: that of sustaining the climax of 450 pages of intense scientific argument. This is the culmination towards which the entire text has been building up. (185–6)

Halliday's functional approach attends to the effects of repetition in a work, the way in which such lexical reverberations signal a cohesive relationship among disparate elements of the text (an effect that rhetoricians since Aristotle have identified). What distinguishes this approach, though, is the way that even the smallest units of discourse – the 'common' words not typically understood as literary – are understood to function in this way; cohesive devices can be conjunctions such as 'and', 'nevertheless', 'so', and 'finally', but they also include terms that 'direct the interpreted elsewhere, either outside or inside the current text, for their interpretation' (Chapman 182). While these words are often pronouns and other forms of reference, they may also be other function words that serve to link elements in the discourse. Applying this method of investigation to dramatic language opens up another level of interpretation, so that a common word can have cumulative effects beyond its individual instances. A good example, and in many ways a quintessential 'common' word, is *will*. Unusually rich in semantic potential, particularly for Shakespeare, *will* can be a proper name and authorial signature, a polysemous noun, and a suggestive and diverse verb. Plentiful evidence in Shakespeare's canon suggests that it is a word he found particularly provocative. He returns to it to puzzle over and play with, perhaps most famously and bawdily in sonnets 135 and 136: 'Will will fulfill the treasure of thy love, / Ay, fill it full with wills, and my will one' (136.5–6). Here, *will*'s punning associations extend to sexual desire, non-sexual desire, male and female sex organs, and, of course, the author's own name.

In *Troilus and Cressida*, too, there is a striking emphasis on the word *will* – at various points in the play, both Ulysses and Troilus offer disquisitions of sorts on what *will* signifies and the complexities embedded within it – and in particular the connotations of *will* as a noun. Ulysses (who, with Thersites, tends to act as the play's commentator on language and its nuances) suggests *will*'s nominal intricacies in his indictment of disproportionate ambition: 'Power into will, will into appetite; / And appetite, an universal wolf, / So doubly seconded with will and power, / Must make perforce an universal prey / And last eat himself up' (1.3.120–4). Ulysses' explanation depends on semantic differences between power, will and appetite; the implication is that these characteristics are similar but distinct. There is twisting and heady logic at work here, but Ulysses seems to suggest an ascending scale of barbarism, so that the intermediate step between realized 'power' and primitive 'appetite' is 'will', a word that walks the tightrope between authority and blindly self-serving desire.[12] In this speech, *will* is presented as a loaded word rife with suggestive potential. Its expressive capacity is reinforced in Act 2 in an exchange between Troilus and Hector, when Hector, in response to Troilus's query 'What's aught but as 'tis valued?' asserts that 'value dwells not in particular will' (2.2.52–3). Troilus's somewhat muddled retort shows him stumbling through the foggy byways of *will*'s various associations:

> I take today a wife, and my election
> Is led on in the conduct of my will,
> My will enkindled by mine eyes and ears,
> Two traded pilots 'twixt the dangerous shores
> Of will and judgement. How may I avoid,
> Although my will distaste what it elected,
> The will I chose?
>
> (2.2.61–7)

Troilus uses *will* as an indicator of desire – 'my will' – and as an agent of choice and decision-making ('will and judgement').

Both meanings dovetail with the modal meanings of *will*: desire in the present moment leads to choices that determine future outcomes. Interestingly, Troilus opposes 'judgement' to 'will'. While his speech clouds the precise differences between the two, it might be presumed given the particular resonance of *will* in the rest of the passage that 'judgement' operates more objectively than 'will', which is tainted by the influence of fickle and mutable desire.

Playing with the same word in different syntactical or grammatical positions is one of Shakespeare's stylistic calling cards, and his puns are often rooted in this type of wordplay: 'Therefore 'tis meet Achilles meet not Hector' (1.3.333); 'Well may we fight for her whom, we know well, / The world's large spaces cannot parallel' (2.2.161–2). These examples use the figure of *antanaclasis*, where a word is repeated with its meaning shifted. In some ways, of course, the practice under discourse analysis to trace the repetition of words in different contexts throughout the discourse is similar to the analysis of repetition and punning through the methods of literary criticism and rhetoric. Shakespeare's conspicuous use of various rhetorical figures of repetition reflect the critical influence of the rhetorical manuals of his age (and, as will be discussed in Chapter 4, the experience of the Tudor grammar school). Yet Halliday's 'lexical cohesion' approach need not be seen simply as a renaming of a classical practice. Rather, it can augment a more traditional rhetorical type of reading in that it highlights not only words with lexical meanings, but also those with specifically grammatical functions. It allows for a wider net to be cast, as in the case of *will* in *Troilus and Cressida*. We understand that *will* is being held up for attention in a particular way through the respective speeches of Ulysses and Troilus (something similar is at work in with the word 'honour' in *Henry V, Part 1*, through the respective reflections of Falstaff and Hotspur). Yet the resonance of *will* in *Troilus and Cressida* extends beyond its nominal instances to encompass its grammatical functions as well. While we don't hear Cressida parsing the finer points of the noun form of *will*, as Ulysses and Troilus do, there is subtle attention cast on her *will* in its modal verb form. As discussed in Chapter 1, modal auxiliary verbs were in transition in early modern English, retaining lingering associations of their lexical meanings while also beginning to act as grammatical markers. Just as the *shall*s at the centre of the analysis of *Coriolanus* in Chapter 1 encode notions of authoritative power, the *will*s of *Troilus and Cressida* retain the potential to designate wishes or desires. As Susan Fitzmaurice has observed, the modal usage of *will* in early modern English is often marked: 'it may be used to express a state of affairs or an event as hoped or wished for ... rather than as stated as actual fact in the future' ('Tentativeness and Insistence' 12).

Given this perspective, and given the fact that the word *will* has already been accented for audiences by Ulysses' and Troilus's respective commentaries, it is telling to pay close attention to speakers' expressions of *will* in *Troilus and Cressida* because they can convey something of the speaker's attitude towards potential future outcomes, particularly the strength of their desire towards that outcome. I do not mean to suggest that Shakespeare approaches *will* as a grammarian would, keen to demonstrate and exemplify all of its possible usages. However, as a playwright attuned to the possibilities contained in individual words, he is alert to the resonance of *will*, and often brings together its disparate forms in suggestive ways. In an emotionally charged moment in the play, Aeneas arrives to inform Troilus, who has just spent the night with Cressida, of the alarming news that Cressida has been traded to the Greeks in an exchange of prisoners. Their respective reactions to the news are notably divergent:

TROILUS
 Is it concluded so?

AENEAS
 By Priam and the general state of Troy.
 They are at hand and ready to effect it.

TROILUS
> How my achievements mock me! –
> I will go meet them. And, my Lord Aeneas,
> We met by chance; you did not find me here.

(4.2.68–73)

Troilus's reaction amounts to a defeatist question and a single statement of mild resistance, followed by immediate compliance – 'I will go' – and erasure: 'you did not find me here'. Compare Cressida's response upon receiving the same news from Pandarus:

CRESSIDA
> O you immortal gods! I will not go.

PANDARUS
> Thou must.

CRESSIDA
> I will not, uncle …
> Tear my bright hair and scratch my praised cheeks,
> Crack my clear voice with sobs, and break my heart
> With sounding 'Troilus'. I will not go from Troy.[13]

(4.2.95–7, 108–10)

Cressida's final, impossible assertion – 'I will not go from Troy' – is a superb example of Shakespeare's deft deployment of striking monosyllables. The difference in their reactions – Troilus's 'will' and Cressida's 'will not' – lays bare their disparate loyalties at this point in the play. Troilus's fidelity is to Troy, while Cressida's is to herself and Troilus.

Later, when Cressida confronts Troilus about her forced departure, his response is curt and unyielding:

CRESSIDA
> I must, then, to the Grecians?

TROILUS
> No remedy.

(4.4.53–4)

Troilus assents with a ready willingness that Cressida cannot fathom, and indeed will not heed until Troilus insists. This conversation, in which each speaker negotiates the news of their reconfigured future, demonstrates a shift in Cressida's speech. To return to the modes of analysis that consider turn-taking and types of utterances, Cressida begins by adopting her typical stance of relative control. She asks questions, in this case about when they may be reunited, and continues to ask even when Troilus is elliptical and avoidant in his responses. They are speaking at cross purposes; while Cressida remains fixated on establishing a reunion, Troilus is stuck on the more abstract point of fidelity.

CRESSIDA
When shall we see again?

TROILUS
Hear me, my love. Be thou but true of heart –

CRESSIDA
I true? How now, what wicked deem is this?
(4.4.56–8)

In the face of Cressida's strong discursive moves – interrogating, interrupting, exclaiming – Troilus responds with his own imperatives and conditions. To her repeated 'when shall I see you?' (4.4.70), he responds 'I will corrupt the Grecian sentinels / To give thee nightly visitation. / But yet, be true' (4.4.71–3). Here, Cressida's discursive power – along with her capacity to determine her own future – begins to fade. Troilus's words reflect a growing rejection of her: he deflects her queries about what will happen to focus on her projected failure of fidelity.

This moment of the play introduces fissures in the relationship between Troilus and Cressida, and there seems to be looming disjunction and separation not only physically, but also in the way that these characters understand one another, their relationship, and their context; the different expressions of *will* here capture this failure of consensus. Their relationship acts as a looming reminder of misunderstanding and troubled interaction in the play, and a primary source of confusion is their failure to understand one another, even at the most basic level of a common understanding of words. In the tense moments following the discovery that Cressida is to be handed over to the Greeks, *will* is the symbol of this failure of consensus:

TROILUS
> But I can tell that in each grace of these
> There lurks a still and dumb-discursive devil
> That tempts most cunningly. But be not tempted.

CRESSIDA
> Do you think I will?

TROILUS
> No.
> But something may be done that we will not;
> And sometimes we are devils to ourselves,
> When we will tempt the frailty of our powers,
> Presuming on their changeful policy.

(4.4.88–96)

The *will*s of this passage are interesting because they expose the potential for different pragmatic intents. Cressida's use of *will* is different from Troilus's, a difference that has significant implications for their interaction, and for the respective parameters that each draws for their relationship. Given the tenor of the exchange up until this point, with Troilus thwarting Cressida's questions, her response reflects frustration and exasperation. Cressida's *will* here emphasizes its modal function, denoting intention, future action and likely outcomes, a sense that sets her *will* at odds with Troilus's. His *will*, in contrast, denotes desire, the dangerously misleading agent that he opposed to judgement in his discussion with Hector. His interpretation is evident in his use of *will* as a main (non-auxiliary) verb, thus fully engaging its semantic associations. He has apparently understood Cressida's question in the same way; that is, as if she has also used *will* as a lexical verb rather than as a modal auxiliary in order to ask *Do you think I want to?* Troilus questions whether she *wants* to do it; Cressida wonders if he thinks that she is *going to* do it. What is intriguing is that Troilus's reaction to Cressida's *will* unwittingly calls out its volitional aspects, and the discrepancies between the *will*s engages the tension between these characters. Troilus insists that Cressida is not as inscrutable as she claims to be, a suspicion that is borne out by the competing *will*s. Even if Cressida is merely trying to discern the future, her desire unavoidably informs the shape of that future. Troilus's use of *will* insists that Cressida claim a sort of culpability that she resists.

Cressida's use of *will* is also interesting because it is unusual; she utters the phrase 'I will' rarely, and consistently at a charged moment in the play.[14] Cressida's reticence seems to contribute to the relative lack of attention given to her side of the story by critics. Yet in the pivotal betrayal scene, Troilus offers an open and extended commentary on what he has beheld, while Cressida slips, troublingly, into offstage silence. All expressions of desire and volition are hidden from us in a letter that remains unread. This gap means that Cressida is often read as a cipher, frustratingly withheld from us 'at exactly the moment at which we most need to understand what [she] is doing' (Adelman, 'This Is and Is Not Cressid' 128).[15] A primary reason that Cressida is obscured from us is her tendency to resist modal assertions; instead, she deflects attention from her own volition by demanding such information from others. In her first interactions with Troilus, for example, her *will*s are oriented exclusively towards him in her repeated invitation, 'Will you walk in, my lord?' (3.2.59, 95). This *will* is in fact Cressida's first word in this scene, and it is telling that it is spoken in reference to the intention of Troilus. Subsequent lines fail to offer any reciprocal declarations of her own will; instead, she maintains the focus on Troilus's intention: 'you will play the tyrant' (3.2.115).

Because Cressida so rarely shares her will, the instances when it is conveyed – invariably forcefully – acquire particular significance. The first vehement instances occur during the scene mentioned above, when she learns that she must decamp to the Greeks: 'O you immortal gods! I will not go' (4.2.95); 'I will not, uncle' (4.2.97); 'I will not go from Troy' (4.2.110).[16] The second set of asserted *will*s occurs with Diomedes, with Troilus looking on: 'I will not meet with you tomorrow night' (5.2.76); 'I will not tell you whose' (5.2.99); and the final, fateful 'I will not keep my word' (5.2.106). These expressions of *will* share a sense of strong intention and defiant wilfulness, examples of how *will* can swerve towards 'obligation' by expressing 'resolve' (Traugott and Dasher 223; Perkins 43). Indeed, the *I will not* usage extends so far into the territory of subjective resolve that it tends to 'express a present state of mind' rather than a reference to the future (Visser 1679). For Cressida, *will* means resolve and resistance, a wall erected against conditions that are being forced upon her. The fervent expression of resolve *I will not* is her sole defence against the order to move to the Greek camp, or to comply with Diomedes' aggressive methods of courting.

Given the context of Cressida's corpus of *will*s in the play, the puzzle of her final betrayal in the play's unsettling fifth act – 'I will not keep my word' (5.2.104) – may be brought into new focus. The strange and discordant forms of communication in *Troilus* reach their apex in Act 5, Scene 2, with its tiers of participants in and observers of dialogue. There is a visual emphasis on separation that is evident on stage; just as the separate tents of the Greeks physically demarcate their partitioned forces, so the factions of spectators in this scene underscore their disconnectedness. The central linguistic event of the scene is the conversation between Cressida and Diomedes, which is partially overheard and reacted to by Troilus and Ulysses, who are themselves observed and scrutinized by the gleefully scopophilic Thersites. The audience, too, is complicit in the chain of covert observation; in fact, we occupy the panoptic place of privilege. The formal details of the scene inscribe a perspective on language that is always, and necessarily, dependent on the observation or participation of others. During a quarrel between Diomedes and Cressida, the shared nature of language is ironically stressed, when Troilus's shadow voice completes the verse line:

> DIOMEDES [*Starts to leave*]
>   And so, good night.
> CRESSIDA   Nay, but you part in anger.
> TROILUS [*aside*]
>   Doth that grieve thee?   O withered truth!
> ULYSSES [*to Troilus, aside*]
>   Why, how now, my lord?
> TROILUS [*to Ulysses, aside*]   By Jove, I will be patient.
> CRESSIDA
>   Guardian! Why, Greek!
> DIOMEDES   Foh, foh! Adieu. You palter.
>   (5.2.47–50)

Here the love triangle is literalized in the act of speaking, a trick that stresses not only the contest between Troilus and Diomedes to claim the position as Cressida's interlocutor/lover, but also the potential for danger and insecurity inherent in something shared, words and lovers alike.

The back-and-forth banter between Cressida and Diomedes – which turns on her teasing refusals to give up the sleeve and playful name-calling: 'O false wench! – Give't me again!' (5.2.73) – displays her characteristic confidence and skill in innuendo. But there are suggestions of resentment in Cressida's speech, and this dialogue recalls her earlier exchanges with Troilus in several key ways. In what sounds like a reprisal of the pivotal 'do you think I will?' moment in Act 4, the differences between *will* as desire (as supposed by Troilus and

Diomedes) and *will* as intention (as supposed by Cressida) are again emphasized:

DIOMEDES
But will you, then?
CRESSIDA
In faith, I will, la. Never trust me else.

(5.2.60–1)

Shortly following this exchange, as she ceases to fight for the sleeve, Cressida seems to articulate her decision in the moment that it is being made: 'Well, well, 'tis done, 'tis past. And yet it is not; / I will not keep my word' (5.2.103–104). This exchange recalls a parallel encounter between Cressida and Troilus in Act 4, when Troilus's words reflect a growing rejection of her: he refuses to satisfy Cressida's queries about what 'will' happen, focuses on her projected failure of fidelity, and demonstrates his willingness to hand her over to the Greeks.[17] The failure of their 'wills' to meet in this scene initiates a fracture that, by the time of Cressida's encounter with Diomedes, plausibly leads to a resistance in Cressida that is now oriented towards Troilus himself. He has rebuffed her, and (in keeping with her expressions of resolve against leaving Troy, and against telling Diomedes the name of her lover) she now resolves herself to a sort of retribution against him. Her move towards estrangement may be seen as 'an act of self-preservation' (Schalkwyk, *Speech and Performance* 165), and the formulation 'I will not' provides the fulcrum.

Halliday's description of discourse as 'texts' is helpful in understanding the failure of cooperation and understanding between Cressida and those with whom she interacts:

> A text is a process of sharing: the shared creation of meaning. Those who share in this process are the 'you' and the 'me' of the text. Our status as co-actants is made explicit in the text itself – in the grammar, which distinguishes between the

speech roles (me and you) on the one hand, and everyone
and everything else (him, her, it, them) on the other. Thus
'you' and 'me' are not only the creators of the text; we are
also created by it. 'You' and 'me' are brought into being by
language. (*Linguistic Studies* 228)

Participants in linguistic exchanges collaborate to create a text, and are in turn remade by it. In this dynamic linguistic process, contributor roles are always in flux, constantly being redefined by the details of the exchange itself: 'Our status as creators and creations of the text is institutionalized by the grammar, and constantly reiterated throughout its proceedings' (229).[18] Much is at stake, then, for the 'co-actants' of communication. In Halliday's vision of exchange between speakers, each takes their turn inhabiting the 'you' and 'me' roles, and they determine and reassess the features of these roles as the interaction moves forward. Halliday's perspective provides an intriguing lens through which to view the climactic moment of fracture for Troilus in the wake of Cressida's betrayal. To his accomplice, Ulysses, Troilus paints the disenchanting events that have unfolded as a disconnect between words and vision:

ULYSSES
  Why stay we, then?
TROILUS
  To make a recordation to my soul
  Of every syllable that here was spoke.
  But if I tell how these two did co-act,
  Shall I not lie in publishing a truth?
  Sith yet there is a credence in my heart,
  An esperance so obstinately strong,
  That doth invert th'attest of eyes and ears,
  As if those organs had deceptious functions,
  Created only to calumniate.
  Was Cressid here?
                                          (5.2.122–31)

Pointing to the 'co-act'ing between Cressida and Diomedes, Troilus provides an apt analogue for Halliday's theory. He further identifies the risks of such an interactive model. If the 'you' and 'me' roles of the exchange are perpetually being remade and even substituted, then what stands as truth between one set of co-actants (or indeed between a momentary incarnation of the 'you'–'me' pairing) can just as easily be a lie between a new set. Cressida's words to Diomedes do not repudiate the ones that she spoke to Troilus, but the conviction remains that he 'shall lie in publishing a truth' (118). This is the rub of co-acting; it is not just the participants that change, but the substance of each encounter is created anew. The cynical assessment of profitless talk made by Troilus in the play's first act – 'PANDARUS: I speak no more than truth. / TROILUS: Thou dost not speak so much' (1.1.61–2) – is illustrated many times over during the course of the play: truth, or even consensus, in interaction is an illusion, as mutable situations of encounter, and variable co-actants, will prove. With Troilus's cynical gloss on the divided Cressida, this entire betrayal scene is provisional and unsettling, a feeling of incompletion captured by Thersites' scene-closing words: 'Lechery, lechery, still wars and lechery; nothing else holds fashion. A burning devil take them!' (5.2.201–203). The self-appointed chorus falters here, choosing to turn away in disgust rather than linger on the discomfiting events that have enfolded. As I hope the discussion in this chapter has suggested, a significant contributor to the unnerving final act of this play is the silencing of Cressida's voice. The methods of discourse analysis help to illuminate her trajectory from active speaker to acted-upon object, underscoring the extent of her transformation and its contribution to the play's closing notes of loss and thwarted wills.

3

Richard II: 'Here, cousin'

Somewhere near the midpoint of *Richard II*, the party accompanying the newly returned exile, Bolingbroke, engages in a telling exchange. As the group approaches Flint Castle, Bolingbroke inquires about the location of his cousin, the king:

NORTHUMBERLAND
  The news is very fair and good, my lord:
  Richard not far from hence hath hid his head.

YORK
  It would beseem the Lord Northumberland
  To say 'King Richard'. Alack the heavy day
  When such a sacred king should hide his head.

NORTHUMBERLAND
  Your grace mistakes; only to be brief
  Left I his title out.

(3.3.5–11)

Northumberland's reply to York's charge of impertinence is clearly disingenuous; the feeble appeal to brevity hardly holds up.[1] His defensiveness reveals that he has touched a nerve, and the title of 'king' that he omits holds the weight of several of this play's central themes: concerns about propriety and legitimacy, as well as questions of obedience and sedition. Like the clamouring voices of *Coriolanus*, the subjects in *Richard II* are driven to 'speak, speak', and with their speech they strive to stake or deny claims to names, land and power. In this climate, the words that signify these contested goals – and the unstable names that are tenuous but significant markers of identity – are crucial, as Northumberland well knows.

One of Shakespeare's most lyrical plays, *Richard II* features an unusally formal style, with 'more rhymes, more declamation and more formally structured speeches such as oaths, curses, lamentations and proclamations than any of the tragedies' (Gurr, 'Textual Analysis' 192). Like *Coriolanus*, *Richard II* holds up for attention the rules and conditions of language use, and particularly the 'social dimensions of meaning' (Siemon 5): the ways in which the subject is constructed and deconstructed in linguistic exchanges. Language-related words proliferate in *Richard II*, especially terms concerning spoken communication such as 'speak', 'speech', 'name', 'tongue' and 'mouth'. As discussed in the Introduction of this book, language is a social phenomenon because it is necessarily contingent, a continuous generative process that unfolds in verbal interaction between speakers. The reciprocity undergirding linguistic encounters is an ongoing source of conflict, both open and covert. The centrality of the social world to the private individual is given particular emphasis in *Richard II*, both in the struggle of its endangered king and in its persistent focus on public spectacle, and the language of this play is consistently aware of its audience and attuned to its performative quality.

The framework of pragmatics, with an emphasis on deixis, offers a productive approach to reading the unstable context of *Richard II*. Deictic markers show us precisely how and when the ground shifts, so to speak, just as they provide essential tools for monitoring how speakers react to a mutable environment. In *Richard II*, the 'common' words with which the imperiled king attempts to position himself demonstrate consistent strategies of resistance against threat and fear. Like the other approaches to language featured in this book, pragmatics places its emphasis on linguistic elements that exist alongside and in tandem with grammar and semantics. Semantic meaning can be thought of as a sort of 'code' to be determined in interpretation, while pragmatic meaning is determined by the context of utterance. Pragmatics may loosely be defined as the study of contextually sensitive meanings, and as such it casts a wide net:

> It is necessary for the adequate account of language that there should be a rigorous study of how language interacts with context – but that study is not in itself strictly a linguistic study. Pragmatics is distinguished from 'core' linguistics by being concerned not just with the linguistic component of the mind but with the much larger set of knowledge and cognitive processes concerned with the interpretation of communication in context. (Chapman 11)

A simpler definition of pragmatics is that it considers the factors that underpin what we say, and a pragmatic analysis necessarily involves reading between the lines to find these unspoken influences. For example, a semantic understanding of 'Can you close the window?' depends on the addressee's understanding of the 'code' behind the verb *close* and the noun *window*, as well as the recognition that such a statement is a request for action. A pragmatic reading, in contrast, considers why and how the speaker is making this request: Is the addressee physically closer to the window than the speaker? What is the relationship between the speaker and the addressee (i.e. is the speaker socially more powerful than the addressee, and thus confident that her request will be met)? Is the request a subtle way for the speaker to indicate that she is cold? These are the types of analyses and judgements that we tend to make unconsciously and unceasingly in the processes of communication. They are so common – and often so unremarkable – that they tend to become invisible. Yet an appreciation of these pragmatic meanings and effects is critical to a complete understanding of how language, and especially dialogue, functions. Pragmatic analysis is particularly apt in the study of dramatic dialogue, which heavily depends on interpersonal conflict and the negotiation of status.

The boundaries of pragmatics are porous and contested. Discourse analysis, for example, may be considered a methodology within the category of pragmatics because it provides tools for the study of context. The discussion of *Coriolanus* in Chapter 1 explored how modality reveals the stance of the self, and showed how monitoring it (particularly during the moments of conflict and threat) can yield rich clues about character attitudes and motivations. In Chapter 2's analysis of *Troilus and Cressida*, I suggest that discourse analysis is a useful approach for determining some pragmatic effects. In this chapter, I shift the emphasis to another branch of pragmatic inquiry that sits adjacent to discourse analysis, and that shares with modality vital information about a speaker's stance and position in the world: the field of deixis. The term 'deixis' is used in linguistics 'to refer to the function of personal and demonstrative pronouns, of tense and a variety of other grammatical and lexical features which relate utterances to the spatio-temporal co-ordinates of the act of utterance' (Lyons, *Semantics* 636). Terms with deictic import such as *I, here, this* and *now* anchor a speaker and an utterance in time and space: they are words that designate location and identity, and are thus vital in gauging external physical position and the inward attitudinal stance of the self. Deictic markers are common words with surprising depth; because their meanings are innately linked to context (i.e. there is no 'code' to tell us who *I* is, separate from the specific context in which it is uttered), they are the rare lexical forms that have in-built pragmatic significance. For this reason – the linking of the subjective and the grammatical in neat monosyllables – deictic markers add subtle depth and momentum to literary language. The force of Gertrude Stein's famous maxim 'There is no there there,' for example, depends on the various shades of meaning that attend the deitic term *there*, and the reader's implicit understanding of *there* as a marker of distance, replete with regret and nostalgia, in addition to its indicative ('there is' ...) and substantive functions. The innate ambiguity of deictic terms like *there* is a boon to poets and dramatists; consider

Lear's enigmatic and puzzled-over final words, 'Look there, look there!' (*KL* 5.3.309). With a slightly different emphasis, John Donne's celebrated opening line 'Mark but this flea' demonstrates how the proximal *this* has the effect of drawing readers into a specific spatial world (complete with its own laws and dimensions), exhorted at once to join the speaker in close relation to the flea, and to his mistress.[2] Shakespeare's eye for the poetic potential of common words extends to deictic markers. Just as he plays on the various meanings of *will* in Sonnets 135 and 136, he relies on the innate ambiguity of *that* and *this*, and their competing associations of distance and affinity, in Sonnet 74: 'The worth of that is that which it contains, / And that is this, and this with thee remains' (13–14).

Critical engagement with deixis first emerged in the field of linguistics, and later moved beyond disciplinary boundaries as linguistics and social scientists with broad interests in anthropology, sociology and philosophy recognized its potential as an important phenomenon that spanned disciplinary boundaries. The French linguist Emile Benveniste, working in the wake of Saussure's landmark *Course in General Linguistics*, posited the centrality of personal pronouns such as *I* and *you* as primordial expression of the self. These deictic indicators are what a speaker use to identify and situate themselves in the world, and in Benveniste's view they act as the progenitors of subjectivity in language. Pronouns are so deeply embedded in our linguistic consciousness that they can go unnoticed, but they are foundational: 'a language without the expression of person cannot be imagined' (225). In the post-structuralist era following the mid-twentieth century, American linguists and anthropologists such as Charles J. Fillmore and William F. Hanks made the study of deixis central to their studies of Indo-European and Mayan languages, respectively. As Hanks notes, deictics are keystone linguistic forms, bringing together various crucial elements of the utterance within one simple word: 'Deictics ground the discourse in which they occur in the broader context of its production, connecting texts to participants, circumstances, and the actual conditions of interaction' (Hanks, *Intertexts* 8). Forms of deixis include personal deixis, which isolates participants in a speech situation in words such as personal pronouns; spatial deixis, which points to the speaker's position in relation to other persons and the world of objects; and temporal deixis, which points to the time of speaking in relation to the utterance and 'to the larger temporal matrix of the world to which both speech situation and what is said belong' (Ruthrof 48). Common to all deictic utterances is the capacity to ground locations and persons in a specific physical context, words which designate the 'identity or placement in space or time of individuated objects relative to the participants in a verbal interaction' (Hanks, *Intertexts* 5). The link to the material world is vital – as the term's origin in the Greek *deiknynai*, 'to display', attests – for the system of deixis is fundamentally indexical, and indexical signs are typically physically connected to their objects.[3]

In 1983, Steven C. Levinson, a social scientist with broad research interests in linguistics and cognition, published the first comprehensive handbook on the study of pragmatics. Levinson's handbook delineated various forms of deixis, and it expanded the field of personal deixis to 'social' or 'attitudinal' deixis, which focuses on the ways in which markers such as personal pronouns indicate degrees of social power, and social distance or intimacy. In literary criticism, and particularly in Shakespeare studies, this form of deixis has received the lion's share of attention. The *thou/you* personal pronominal system was a 'primary grammatical tool for expressing social distance and intimacy' in early modern English (Fitzmaurice, *Familiar Letter* 44), and a number of studies over the past several decades have traced the effects of these pronouns in Shakespeare's dramatic dialogue.[4] Others have extended the study of distance and intimacy to additional elements of social deixis. Susan Fitzmaurice, for example, productively traces deictic patterns in selected early modern letters to show how epistolary interlocutors negotiate social status and intimacy within the private discourse of the letter. Keir Elam's foundational work *The Semiotics of Theatre and Drama,* published in 1980, posited deictic phenomena as central to drama, and it remains a key resource for scholarship of deixis in drama. Over a decade later, Vimala Herman's research on dramatic language opened up important new avenues for the discussion of deixis, particularly in its application to Shakespeare.[5] More recently, Heather Dubrow has considered spatial deixis in the context of early modern lyric poetry in an approach that combines close pragmatic reading with attention to broader cultural and generic developments.

The relationship between speaker, space, and context that deictic terms establish – the ability to indicate the literal stance of a speaker in the world – reflects a parallel to the modal expressions discussed in previous chapters. Just as modality establishes the uniqueness of a speaker's perspective, deictic markers measure the position of speakers relative to their interlocutors, settings, and utterances. In this way, deictic terms of reference are the *origo* of expressions of identity, the very 'expressions of person' that Benveniste views as fundamental to subjectivity in language (225).[6] As Lyons explains, because deictic terms use the spatial position – and indeed the physical body – of the speaker as their point of origin, they are fundamentally egocentric:

> The speaker, by virtue of being the speaker, casts himself in the role of ego and related everything to his viewpoint. He is at the zero-point of the spatio-temporal coordinates of what we will refer to as the deictic context. Egocentricity is temporal as well as spatial, since the role of speaker is being transferred from one participant to the other as the conversation proceeds, and the participants may move around as they are conversing: the spatio-temporal zero-point (the here-and-now) is determined by the place of the speaker at the moment of utterance. (*Semantics* 638)

The inextricable link between deictic terms and the speaker, as well as to what Lyons calls the 'situation-of-utterance', means that deixis has particular currency in spoken language. In fact, increased frequency of deictic markers is a distinguishing and quantifiable feature of verbal interaction: 'The percentage of deictic terms tends to be much higher in conversation than in literature, as one could guess: speech is egocentric, and speakers continually define their position relative to their listeners' (Furrow 366). Predictably, the literary 'conversations' that comprise dramatic speech display a remarkably high percentage of deictic terms. The centrality of deixis to dramatic language is twofold: first because of its role in establishing the speaker positions and relationships between characters, and second because it alludes to the imagined physical and temporal environment of the stage, the *this* and *that* of the immediate stage context, or the *now* that posits an instant of dramatic time unique to that moment on stage.[7] Elam suggests that deixis is, in fact, 'the most significant linguistic feature – both statistically and functionally – in the drama' (27).

The fundamental link between deixis and the physical body is another reason that it is so relevant to the analysis of dramatic language. We tend to think of language as primarily cerebral, but deixis lays bare the link between the linguistic and the corporeal. Deixis draws together three discrete strands that are central to dramatic language: grammar (since terms like *I* and *now* comprise the 'common' foundational words of the language), subjectivity (because they serve as an expression of how speakers position themselves in the world), and the physical body (which provides the deictic centre, or point of origin). Gestural deictic moments like a touch of the crown or a knee to the ground make tangible the point of contact between the subject/speaker and the world around him.

Although deictic reference is highly particularized and intimately linked to the speaker, it is necessarily framed by a dynamic context of interaction. Therefore the claim that deixis is 'egocentric', while not incorrect, is rather limiting because it closes off the interactive and socially embedded reality of deictic speech. As Fitzmaurice explains, 'the fact that deixis is centred on the speaker and the speaker's location invites the assumption that it is both inherently subjective and egocentric.

However, as a system that cannot define the subject ... except in relation to the position of others, it might be constructed as social rather than subjective, and as empathetic rather than egocentric' (*Familiar Letter* 41). My analysis in this chapter stresses the interactive aspect of deixis, and follows Hanks in regarding it as 'a social construction, central to the organization of communicative practice and intelligible only in relation to a sociocultural system' (*Intertexts* 5). Most important is the idea that seemingly benign words such as *I* and *this* bear the weight of social bonds, because they are grounded in the relation between speech participants. Deictic utterances are not generically transferable across contexts; rather, their nuances vary according to the situation, and to the relationship between interlocutors. The situational frameworks in which deictic terms are employed hold sway over their execution, for speakers vary deictic reference according to factors such as the relative status of their addressee. 'When speakers say "Here it is"', Hanks attests, 'he/she unavoidably conveys something like "Hey, you and I stand in a certain relation to each other and to this object and this place, right now"' (*Referential Practice* 7). Because the circumstances of this relation are always in flux, speakers continually renegotiate and re-establish their position from moment to moment. The necessary variability that undergirds the system of deixis intensifies the dramatic power of one of *Richard II*'s most famous passages. When John of Gaunt, the fact of his imminent death designating him a 'prophet new inspired' (2.1.31), laments the state of his country – 'This royal throne of kings, this sceptered isle, / This earth of majesty, this seat of Mars, / This other Eden ... This fortress built by Nature for herself ... This happy breed of men, this little world, / This precious stone set in the silver sea ... This blessed plot, this earth, this realm, this England' (2.1.40–50) – the anaphoric 'this' bears a heavy expressive burden. Gaunt's insistent 'this' is a drum beat of proximity: his audience is reminded with each line that the very ground upon which they stand is sacred and imperiled. The urgency is redoubled by Gaunt's unstable position at the threshold between life and death; for now, he occupies a corporeal centre from which to speak, from which to mark his proximity to the land, but this position is fleeting. His deictic markers reinforce to his listeners the urgency to protect 'this England', here and now.

The title of 'king' certainly bears a conspicuously heavy burden of social signification, and in *Richard II* it is marked to an even greater degree by the fact that it changes hands – or, more fittingly, heads; the king who wears the crown as the play opens is not the king of the play's final act. 'King' is compelling from a deictic perspective because it is a specialized name to which only one individual can justly lay claim, while at the same time it is a social signifier of the highest order. Yet what is interesting about 'king' in *Richard II* is the mutable context of its usage. Since deictic terms, including titles, derive from specific contexts, what happens when the ground symbolically shifts, as it does so decisively in *Richard II*? Hanks suggests that contexts are 'crosscut by conflicting subcontexts for the same words, so that not all example usages can be explained by the same semantic representation' (*Language and Communicative Practice* 83). *Richard II* demonstrates the extent to which a specialized context can destabilize semantic representation. 'King' to Richard is not simply a title, nor merely an inhabitable persona, but rather an absolute identity. Deprived of it, he has 'no name, no title – / No, not that name was given me at the font – / But 'tis usurped. Alack the heavy day, / That I have worn so many winters out / And know not now what name to call myself' (4.1.255-9).

In *Richard II*, names – their meanings, proper use and social significance – are the objects of much explicit attention, as well as linguistic play. The category of honorifics, or titles of address, fall under the rubric of social deixis, which marks the conditions of the social situation in which the utterance occurs. Markers of social deixis grammaticalize social distinctions so that the parameters of the relationship are encoded in the words themselves (Levinson 89). In *Richard II*, characters repeatedly insist on titles and pun on nominal associations, but at the same time the abundance of names in the dialogue and the recurrent manipulation of honorifics affirm an attention to names that pervades different levels of language from the obvious to the covert. It is evident from the play's opening lines that names will be of particular concern. Flanked by nobles and attendants, Richard offers a virtual catalogue of names to commence the dramatic action:

KING RICHARD
>Old John of Gaunt, time-honoured Lancaster,
>Hast thou according to thy oath and band
>Brought hither Henry Hereford, thy bold son,
>Here to make good the boist'rous late appeal –
>Which then our leisure would not let us hear –
>Against the Duke of Norfolk, Thomas Mowbray?

GAUNT
>I have, my liege.

KING RICHARD
>Tell me, moreover, hast thou sounded him
>If he appeal the Duke on ancient malice,
>Or worthily, as a good subject should,
>On some known ground of treachery in him?
>
>(1.1.1–11)

As king, Richard exercises his authority as the master of naming, the one permitted to bestow and revoke titles. He is as capable of familiarity – 'Old John of Gaunt' – as he is of formality: 'the Duke of Norfolk'. As his audience – both on stage and off – understands all too well, these names can be withheld just as easily as they are conferred. Richard's opening words offer a dubious welcome into a world where names have the paradoxical quality of being superfluous, easily jettisoned and exchanged, while also curiously vital and worth the risks of sedition. Also telling in this opening exhange are King Richard's subtly shifting terms of self-reference. His first questions to Gaunt are framed within the authority of the specialized form of self-reference reserved for the king:

'Which then *our* leisure would not let *us* hear.' Yet after Gaunt responds, in appropriately deferential terms, Richard moves to the standard personal pronoun 'Tell *me*, moreover.' Gaunt is both his subject and his uncle, and the indistinct boundary between King Richard's role as sovereign and his position as a common man who 'live[s] with bread' (3.2.175) like even the 'puny subject[s]' (3.2.86) he commands is a continued source of friction in the play.

In addition to Richard, who frequently invokes his royal title and the presumed power that it represents – 'Is not the King's name twenty thousand names? / Arm, arm, my name!' (3.2.85–6) – other characters regularly allude to and play on their names and titles. John of Gaunt exhausts the pun in a chiasmus-inflected speech responding to Richard's perfunctory inquiry into the health of 'aged Gaunt': 'O, how that name befits my composition! / Old Gaunt indeed, and gaunt in being old ... Gaunt am I for the grave, gaunt as a grave, / Whose hollow womb inherits naught but bones' (2.1.73–4, 83–4). Bolingbroke, for his part, is a nominal chameleon, variously assuming 'Hereford', 'Bolingbroke', 'Derby', 'Lancaster', and ultimately 'Henry, of that name the fourth' (4.1.113). Moreover, he is attuned to the significance of specific names and titles – hardly interchangeable labels, they embody entire identities: 'As I was banished, I was banished Hereford; / But as I come, I come for Lancaster' (2.3.113–14). York displays a similar sensitivity, chiding Bolingbroke for using a name to signify what he deems to be a corrupted identity: 'Tut, tut! / Grace me no grace, nor uncle me no uncle. / I am no traitor's uncle ... ' (2.3.86–8). These examples suggest an intriguing feature of naming that applies to deictic phenomena on a wider scale: its orientation is both egocentric and social. At the same time that names register a highly individual significance – identity and current position – they also inscribe the contingent nature of social relationships. 'Variations in forms of address, notably titles and names, are conventionally used to designate social relationships on the one hand and to capture social attitudes towards and social consideration for addressees on the other'; nominal signifiers are significant indicators of matters of 'relative social status and power, or interpersonal intimacy or distance between actors' (Fitzmaurice, *Familiar Letter* 43). So when York refuses the title of 'uncle' to Bolingbroke, he resists the identity for himself while at the same time he reframes his relationship with Bolingbroke.

The manipulation of honorifics is a common practice in *Richard II*, and as the exchange between York and Northumberland suggests, the strategy gains special significance when applied to claimants to the title of king. Tracking the usage of names in moments of particular tension, as in the mutedly antagonistic encounter between Bolingbroke and Richard at Flint Castle, yields compelling information about how these adversaries position themselves and view one another. Upon learning that Richard is inside the castle, Bolingbroke directs his men in characteristically frank and potent language: 'Go to the rude ribs of that ancient castle; / Through brazen trumpet send the breath of parley / Into his ruined ears, and thus deliver: / Henry Bolingbroke / On both his knees doth kiss King Richard's hand / And sends allegiance and true faith of heart / To his most royal person' (3.3.32–8). Bolingbroke's words carry an understated rhetorical force grounded in his exploitation of honorifics. The line breaks here emphasize the name 'Henry Bolingbroke', bare of any title but commanding in its isolation. Moreover, the inversion of 'thus deliver' immediately preceding the name produces an interesting syntactic effect. The line is rather awkwardly end-stopped by the transitive verb 'deliver', thereby creating an expectation of a direct object to complete its meaning. The name 'Henry Bolingbroke' serves as a phantom object for this verb, so that while the meaning according to the syntactical logic of the lines is that the nobles 'deliver' this message, there remains a subtle echo that it is Bolingbroke himself – the authority behind the name – who will be forcefully 'delivered' into the castle's 'ruined' ears, an apt warning of what is to come.[8] The stark, untitled name is further highlighted by the invocation of 'King Richard' in the subsequent line, and indeed four additional times in the subsequent thirty lines. As it is repeated, the honorific 'King Richard' begins to resemble an exaggerated incantation, and its progression – 'King Richard's hand' (36); 'King Richard's land' (47); 'Methinks King Richard and myself should meet' (54); 'mark King Richard how he looks' (61); 'See, see, King Richard doth himself appear, / As doth the blushing discontented sun / From out the fiery portal of the east' (62–4) – works as a virtual checklist of what Bolingbroke stands poised to take from Richard: his reigning body, his land, the exchange of power and his commanding celestial presence. The relationship of respectful deference between subject and monarch that is encoded in the use of the honorific 'King' is thus undercut. Bolingbroke's excessive repetition, paired with the audacious presentation of his own untitled name in the guise of an authoritative honorific, serves to hollow out the title of 'King' and renders its union with the name 'Richard' an empty signifier.

While Bolingbroke's language in this scene works to undo the relationship between sovereign and subject encoded in the title of 'King', Richard's upholds the monarchical precedent. When he begins to speak, Richard sounds like the quintessential king: 'We are amazed, and thus long have we stood / To watch the fearful bending of thy knee / Because we thought ourself thy lawful king' (3.3.72–4). The engine of Richard's kingly authority is found in his deictic markers, chiefly his pronouns. From his first word, the royal plural 'we', he exercises the monarch's right to a specialized mode of self-reference. As king, he lays claim to a singular deictic code, as evidenced in the unusual reflexive pronoun 'ourself'. This word – one 'self' made double through the plural possessive 'our' – crystallizes in grammar the notion of the king's plural bodies, physical and metaphysical. Employing such pronouns is a privilege unique to the king; not only does such a marker give the impression of a delegation of power that extends beyond one man, it also echoes the self-assured language that Richard tends to favour at the beginning of the play, before his kingship is in imminent jeopardy. His first appearances in the play show him as decisively regal, flanked by supporters (as of yet ostensibly compliant) and skilfully performing of the part of monarch, a role which provides visual clout even in the increasing absence of actual influence. In this passage, Richard begins to waver, his words offering a virtual monitor of his crumbling self-perception. After maintaining the plural pronouns for a few lines – 'For well we know no hand of blood and bone / Can gripe the sacred handle of our sceptre' (3.3.79–80) – he becomes more agitated, spits out the aggressive verbs 'profane, steal or usurp' (81), and slips for a moment: 'Yet know: my master, God omnipotent, / Is mustering in His clouds on our behalf / Armies of pestilence' (85–7). This is a telling departure: although Richard recovers the royal 'our' quickly, he has spoken of God as '*my* master'. Richard's appeal to divine preservation is his best defence; if he is ruler by divine right, then his redemption from Bolingbroke's threat hinges on God's power alone. That he uses a universal mode of self-reference, the singular pronoun 'my', to appeal to this power (even as he issues threats of biblical proportions) may be read as indicative of alarm or desperation. The fear only becomes more pronounced as Richard ratchets up both his threats and the references to himself as utterly human and solitary:

> they shall strike
> Your children, yet unborn and unbegot,
> That lift your vassal hands against my head
> And threat the glory of my precious crown.
> Tell Bolingbroke – for yon methinks he stands –
> That every stride he makes upon my land
> Is dangerous treason.
>
> (3.3.87–93)

These are thrilling lines, ringing with combative energy, yet they harbour an unsteadiness that belies their monitory tone. The extended departure from the kingly plural here registers the extent to which Richard feels threatened. The features that are most endangered – his land, his crown and his head – are those which have been ostentatiously marked by Bolingbroke as belonging to 'King Richard', and are here marked with the more proprietary but less authoritative 'my'. In one sense, Richard's shift in pronouns may be a countering retort to the apparent derision that underlies Bolingbroke's repeated 'King Richard'. By using 'my', Richard signals that the title of 'King' is not as hollow as Bolingbroke hopes; the role is claimed, Richard's pronoun asserts, by one with proprietary claims on the rights of kingship. His reference to 'my land' suggests a defensive territoriality not conveyed by earlier expressions of patriotic ownership such as 'our England' (1.4.35).[9] As Richard's pronouns show, this is not merely a showdown between king and subject; the stakes in this battle are personal. At the same time, however, this usage registers Richard's anxiety. As his threats grow more spectacular, his self-reference grows more personal, as if he has glimpsed the 'unkinged' self that Bolingbroke's sedition threatens to uncover. From a pragmatic perspective, personal pronouns act as gauges of a speaker's emotional state. In this moment of *Richard II*, we witness the unravelling of Richard's composure, and the forced renegotiation of his self-perception, as it happens. Richard's toggling pronouns expose his growing fear at the same time that they expose a shift in his social standing and power. Levinson asserts that 'there is no such thing as a socially neutral form of address' (*Pragmatics* 92), a claim that may be extended to forms of self-address. A change in self-reference is a primary indicator that the ground has shifted; it indicates a movement towards a new 'zero-point' based on the redefined perspective and position of the subject.

Unlike some other forms of address, however, 'king' is hardly a universal subject position. The changing nature of Richard's social standing is necessarily complicated by his royal role. Questions of kingship propel *Richard II*, from concerns about the legitimate scope of monarchical power to the nature of the burden endured by the man who occupies this vaunted position. Often, Richard's words betray an urge to play it both ways: while he refuses to mitigate his royal perogative, he also professes a desire to be understood as feebly human. Despite his canny pleas to be regarded as a common citizen – 'For you have but mistook me all this while. / I live with bread like you, feel want, / Taste grief, need friends. Subjected thus, / How can you say to me I am a king?' (3.2.174–7) – there is no mistaking that he is not a 'subject' in any ordinary sense. Occupying a singular position, a person whose relative health informs the health of an entire nation, the king has a unique type of power; while social power is heavily context-driven, the role of king tends to be fixed, or at least much less vulnerable to change. The speaker at the apex of social power has a peculiar freedom to insist upon their own wishes, and Richard's overt disregard for civil law demonstrates the extent to which he exploits this privilege. As he prepares to claim Bolingbroke's assets, Richard remarks 'Think what you will, we seize into our hands / His plate, his goods, his money, and his lands' (2.1.209–10), explicitly overturning the 'will' of others so that he may fill his own 'hands'. Furthermore, he depends on the apparent inviolability of his role to protect him, for as the Bishop of Carlisle demands, 'What subject can give sentence on his king? / And who sits here that is not Richard's subject?' (4.1.122–3). The position of king relative to his subjects is a heightened example of what linguists identify as role-sets, such as 'manager/employee' or 'parent/child', where 'asymmetrical power is built in' (Brown and Levinson 78). According to these terms, the role-set of 'king/subject' represents an extreme instance of disproportionate power, for the king represents the highest point on the scale of relative social power. In a system where he is the 'head', all designations of power are determined relative to him. But extreme or crisis situations can shift or reverse power even within the starkest hierarchies. Such reversals are at the heart of *Richard II*, and they capture the dilemma of Richard as well as those responsible for overturning the typical role-set, the insurgents who destabilize a network of social power. Though Richard and his supporters may trust in the rigidity of this model of power, the play persists in exposing their faith as naïve.[10] *Richard II* details not only the effects of a reversal of power, but also the process by which even seemingly sacrosanct social power is undermined.

In this scenario, all players in the dramatic world are caught in an intermediate zone where the king occupies a peculiar and transient social space, and the absolute determiners of power no longer hold currency.

Richard's common words can easily be obscured by his overwrought speech, as in a characteristic utterance when he frames his situation in imagistic and quasi-religious terms:

> So, when this thief, this traitor, Bolingbroke,
> Who all this while hath revelled in the night
> Whilst we were wand'ring with the Antipodes
> Shall see us rising in our throne, the east,
> His treasons will sit blushing in his face ...
> Not all the water in the rough rude sea
> Can wash the balm off from an anointed king;
> The breath of worldly men cannot depose
> The deputy elected by the Lord.
>
> (3.2.47–57)

Richard's prediction that Bolingbroke 'shall see us rising in our throne' carries the conviction of a king who is accustomed to having his version of the future fulfilled; his assertion that no water 'can wash the balm from an anointed king', that he 'cannot' be deposed, harnesses the notion of a power greater than his own control. As *can* denotes, such an event is unthinkable because it is beyond the ability of any human or natural force. Such assurance is to be expected from Richard. Herman suggests that 'power in action is power to control consequences of speech, to control the sequels to one's illocutionary acts, and to bend others' actions to one's word and will' (*Dramatic Discourse* 216), and the future-determining power represented by *shall* seems an inherent privilege of kingship. Richard's common words here and elsewhere may easily be overlooked as simple functional components supporting his stylish rhetoric, but it is interesting to track their fluctuation during the moments when his crown, and his identity as monarch, are in jeopardy. Here, I would like to pause on the details of his formal, ritualized language, for the linguistic conditions of ritual offer a meaningful bridge between Richard's characteristic grand language and the banal details of his speech that reveal the defensive processes of a self in crisis. Like the naming rights coveted by the speakers in this play, acts of ritual engage the border between individual and social that is persistently highlighted in *Richard II*. The denotative and connotative values of names cut in various directions, pointing to a highly personal identity while at the same time representing the social relationship between the namer and the named. The language of ritual has a similarly dual nature; in one sense, it is the most public of discourses, embedded in social commentary and spectacle. Rituals comment on the cultural configurations from which they emerge: 'by breaking off and doing something special, set apart, the "discontinuum" of action among the same collection of people, culturally made possible by setting aside times and places for cultural performances, is equally part of the ongoing social process' (Turner 22).[11] Yet while ritual is inextricably tied to the social, it is also highly personal, for the speaker in ritual occupies a central and separate role. The language of ritual, anchored in the body, emphasizes the speaker as a discrete individual. Set apart from but intimately related to the quotidian social world, ritual is a site of assessment and interpretation, but it is also a source of solace during moments of threat.[12]

King Richard regularly turns to the comforting framework of ritual as a source of control in the face of failing efficacy, as witnessed in the early conflict between Bolingbroke and Mowbray. During the initial dispute, Richard attempts to channel regal command: 'Wrath-kindled gentleman, be ruled by me: / Let's purge this choler without letting blood. / This we prescribe, though no physician' (1.1.152–4). His directive is summarily ignored as Mowbray and Bolingbroke reject Richard's conditions of arbitration. It is hardly surprising, for Richard's attempts at commanding language falter: he demands that his subjects submit to his 'rule', but then employs the leniently inclusive 'let's'; he claims the power to 'prescribe', but with the same breath – 'though no physician' – undermines his authority to do so. His subsequent 'We were not born to sue but to command, / Which since we cannot do to make you friends' (1.1.196–7) is an exemplary self-cancelling statement: 'cannot' concedes that it is not within his ability nor his control to accomplish what he was ostensibly 'born' to do. Armed with this failure of command, Richard orders a subsequent meeting in which action, not words, will be the focus: 'At Coventry upon Saint Lambert's Day. / There shall your swords and lances arbitrate / The swelling difference of your settled hate' (1.1.199–201). Yet in the midst of the exhilarating pre-battle moments at Coventry – combatants prepared and trumpets sounding – Richard throws down his warder, severing the anticipatory tension and proving himself a masterful scene-stealer. In one sense, it is a divertive bid for control; his interference shows that he 'accepts the feudal order when it suits him, and jettisons it when he is in danger of losing control over events' (Iser 72). Because it pre-empts any defiant response from Bolingbroke and Mowbray, the disruption is an effective way of ensuring that these 'wrath-kindled gentlemen' are, after all, 'ruled' by him. Some commentators have suggested that this display demonstrates the extent to which Richard degrades the office of kingship, the profound violation that is implied when 'the King, the custodian of order, has himself broken the order of formal occasion' (Leggatt, *Shakespeare's Political Drama* 61).[13] But there is more at stake here than Richard's stubborn insistence on his own way, for the means by which he attempts to regain control seem calculatedly apt. First, by insisting on a ritual that he subsequently breaks, Richard in fact continues the pattern of self-undoing that is evident in his speech. Here, the undermining is more spectacular, and more effective. The interruption of ceremony repositions Richard as the master namer, in control of communicative practices even as his verbal strategies fail him.

Herman argues that, with this move, Richard's objective is cunning redirection rather than straightforward disruption:

'the point of Richard's maneuver is to re-define, re-reference, the proceedings in such a way as to turn the public and constitutional issue of treason into something more trivial and domestic' (*Dramatic Discourse* 216). Richard's urge to 're-define' the ceremony is worth closer examination. We have already seen that Richard, as king, lays claim to an individualized type of language (exemplified by the king-specific pronoun 'ourself'), and that this language often fails to serve him adequately. The signified 'king' that stands as the authority behind these words has already begun to unhinge. Given this framework of failing verbal efficacy, Richard's re-definition of ceremony offers a substitute, a type of individualized language that is rooted in the more polysemous language of the body. 'The language of the body, whether articulated in gestures or ... in what psychosomatic medicine calls "the language of the organs," is incomparably more ambiguous and more overdetermined than the most overdetermined uses of ordinary language' (Bourdieu 120).[14] Richard's act here is not a straightforward violation of ceremony; rather, it is a re-creation of the ritual according to his own laws. The scene retains key components of ritual, the 'breaking off and doing something special, set apart, the "discontinuum" of action' that Turner points to as ritual's defining feature (22). Richard's act of disruption may in fact heighten the ritualistic aspect of the scene, since it thwarts the expected course of events, creating an event that is even more marked and 'set apart'. Moreover, Richard's actions here rely on the physical objects that are universal to ritual, providing the heady visual impact of the warder striking the ground.[15] Understood through the frame of deixis, the act of throwing the warder is especially significant. For just as the physical body is instrumental in ritual – as Hanks notes, 'an important part of occupying the ritual frame is to be corporeally located within it' (*Intertexts* 232) – it is also the grounding zero-point of deictic reference. The throwing of the staff not only places Richard in the centre of the action, the hub of his own redefined ritual; it is also a means of expanding corporeal space. The warder extends the limits of Richard's physical body so that he virtually spreads himself out, inhabiting a wider deictic centre and laying claim to an influence that is both physically and symbolically larger.

Richard regularly demonstrates his tactic of 're-defining' and 're-referencing' ritual at moments when he is threatened. Throwing down the warder before the fight between Mowbray and Bolingbroke provides him with an alternative means to expand his monarchical presence and to guarantee that he will 'rule' one way or another. In this case, the authority of the visual compensates for the gap left by failing verbal power, but there are several other instances when Richard also exploits the rigid and specialized conditions of ritual language. Just as the act of ritual is at once derived from and embedded in ordinary social life, the language of ritual bears an interesting reciprocal relationship to 'ordinary' language. In one sense, ritualized language features inbuilt limitations; as Berger suggests, it 'establishes ground rules that limit the range of possible responses, conspicuously mask "real" feelings and motives beneath sanctioned artificial replacements, and transfer authority from the speakers themselves to their ceremonial roles' (Berger 54). But such limitations are apparent (albeit in a less prescribed way) in all forms of social language. Brown and Levinson suggest that the language of high cultural ritual displays the 'same minutiae of symbolic expression that we find in verbal politeness', and propose that ritualized linguistic interaction exists on a continuum of sorts, so that there is 'a natural continuum from the prototype familial interpersonal rituals, through the elaborate interpersonal rituals of adult life to the highly cathected sacred rites' (44). Moreover, there is a critical relationship between ritual and control. Citing the similarities between verbal politeness (which can often take the form of 'interpersonal ritual') and the 'grand rites' of formal ritual, Brown and Levinson note the importance of the 'role of ritual in social control' and posit links between verbal politeness and political control 'through the constraints it imposes on next actions by addressees' (47). In other words, interpersonal linguistic exchanges and the grand rites of ritual are interconnected: both involve similar constraints and expectations on the part of participants, and the overlap between the two is exploited in *Richard II*.

During the confrontation at Flint Castle, as Richard begins to apprehend the real threat to his throne posed by Bolingbroke, he engages the safety of ritualized language to protect himself. After exposing the fear behind the menace in accusing Bolingbroke of 'dangerous treason' (3.3.93), Richard collapses into a lament that articulates a momentous crisis of identity at the same time that it channels performative power and plays to its audience: 'O God, O God ... O, that I were as great / As is my grief, or lesser than my name! / Or that I could forget what I have been, / Or not remember what I must be now! / Swell'st thou, proud heart? I'll give thee scope to beat, / Since foes have scope to beat both thee and me' (3.3.133, 136–41). Buried in the rhetoric – the plaintive 'O' the opposition of 'great/lesser' and 'forget/remember', the subjunctive tenor of yearning for the impossible – there is a sharp insight. He claims to want an identity separate from 'what I have been' as well as from 'what I must be now'. What Richard longs for is an in-between state, a threshold between identities, and, interestingly, his language here creates it for him. Richard succeeds, however conditionally, in carving out an intermediate space for himself, just beyond the reach of his persecutors and the encroaching alternative world that they represent.

He has abandoned all pretence of royal pronouns, referring to himself exclusively as 'I', and this *I* is uprooted, anchored neither in a 'name' nor in a past or present identity. The *I* is not even grounded in his body, as his appeal to his beating heart, separate from himself, makes clear. Thus the *I* becomes an unmoored signifier, an apt move in preparation for the lines that follow:

What must the King do now? Must he submit?
The King shall do it. Must he be deposed?
The King shall be contented. Must he lose
The name of King? I' God's name, let it go.

(3.3.143–6)

Richard's words bear the accent of ritual: the formality, the repetition, and the call-and-response format recall the pattern of liturgy, and the ceremony at hand appears to be the anointing of a new self. Richard revisits the subject position of 'king' in a slightly skewed way, not by means of a plural pronoun, but through the third person. He invokes the play's most contested title, but now it is tenuously rather than absolutely tied to his own speaker position. Viewed through the lens of deixis, this strategy is intriguing. We have seen how Richard can expand his deictic 'zero-point', the space that he occupies and from which his speaking self is based, in tense moments such as the warder scene. Here, he does the opposite, retreating into a contracted deictic centre. In dialogue – and particularly in dramatic dialogue – certain speaker positions are privileged over others. As Elam explains, 'a central position is occupied by those deictics relating to the context-of-utterance (I-you-here-now), which serve as an indexical "zero-point" from which the dramatic world is defined. In particular, it is on the "pronominal drama" between the I-speaker and the you-listener/addressee that the dramatic dialectic is constructed. "I" and "you" are the only genuinely active roles in the dramatic exchange' (142–3). By withdrawing from the active *I* role and transforming himself into the third-person 'king', thereby positioning himself as 'an excluded and non-participant other presented merely as object of discourse' (Elam 143), Richard effectively takes himself out of the linguistic exchange. The modal verb *shall* in this line is also pertinent; holding the force of an imposed duty, it mandates obedience and eliminates the possibility for agentive choice. Yet Richard's substitution of 'I' for 'king' creates the possibility of a remaining, separate Richard who may defy this obligation. Throughout the play, despite his frequent use of the monarch's future-determining *shall*, Richard never applies this word to himself in the grammatical construction *I shall*. The idea of forced future action, something that obeys the mandate of duty rather than desire, seems to be anathema to him. These recurring statements of what 'the King shall do' are the closest Richard ever comes to declaring that his behaviour will accord with what others have dictated for him, and even here his slippery self-reference grants him a loophole. Richard has achieved the in-between speaker stance that he wished for a few brief lines earlier; his third-person avoidance strategy permits him to momentarily escape the obligations of the king and to 'forget' what he has been.

The anxiety of Richard's position lies in the inevitable recognition that those obligations remain even when the name is lost. Following the self-command to 'let it go', Richard finally takes up the self-reference that is general to all speakers: 'I'll give my jewels for a set of beads, / My gorgeous palace for a hermitage' (3.3.147–8). Stepping into the *I* position represents the assumption of responsibility. Because the utterance of *I* locates the speaker as the 'generating axial centre ... a plotting of the person on a time/space continuum in the precise instance of speech' (Hanafi 93), Richard at once positions himself as *origo* and implicates himself in all aspects of the utterance. As Adamson notes, '"I" is both deictic and pronominal, standing simultaneously for the agent and the referent of discourse, for both narrator and character' ('Emphatic Deixis' 204). And indeed, for Richard, the *I* will represent both agent and victim, a paradoxical position that is also captured in the modals of his cryptic statement of reasoning, spoken directly to his 'Cousin', Bolingbroke: 'What you will have, I'll give, and willing too; / For do we must what force will have us do' (3.3.204–206). The lines toggle between two of Richard's modes of self-reference – the relinquishing 'I' and the coerced 'we' – just as they play on the border of volition and compulsion. The first line emphasizes the volitional quality of *will*, but progresses from Bolingbroke's desire ('what you will have') to a contracted statement of future action ('I'll give'), to end on an adjectival stress on Richard's own volition ('and willing too'). He transforms what amounts to a promise of compliance into a statement about his own act of will, an agency that is neatly reframed in the line that follows. 'For do we must': these four short syllables each encode an explosive assertion. 'For' invokes a causal relationship with the line preceding – the reason for Richard's willingness, it turns out, is the dictate of 'force'. 'Do we must' is an interesting syntactic inversion that places primary stress on the verb, lessening the impact of his shrewd reversion to the royal 'we'. Again, Richard uses logical reasoning to showcase the absurdity of his situation: no mere human volition can dictate what the king 'must do', and what Bolingbroke 'wills' is a consideration only due to the 'force' that commands at this moment. The scene ends with a powerful declaration of acknowledgement – 'Then I must not say no' (3.3.210) – in which Richard simultaneously decrees and acquiesces to the command that he had previously deferred. Richard's fluctuating self-reference and modal choices in this scene preserve his agency at the same time that they indict Bolingbroke for his treachery.

The tendencies in Richard's visual and verbal forms of communication – his bids to be master of symbols and to create a specialized identity through his language – converge in spectacular fashion during the deposition scene in Act 4. Summoned by his persecutors, Richard enters with the air of an in-between monarch: he remains flanked by attendants, but here they act as impersonal sentinels of the kingship. '*[with Officers bearing the crown and sceptre]*' (sd), they hold the royal paraphernalia close to Richard but out of his grasp. The first words spoken by Richard are characteristically incisive. He recognizes the power of his accusers as overseers of the proceedings, and so begins with a question that acknowledges their control, and indeed the relinquished title: 'Alack, why I am sent for to a king / Before I have shook off the regal thoughts / Wherewith I reigned?' (4.1.163–5). Yet he quickly turns the advantage to himself by not waiting for a response, but proceeding in his familiar pattern of ritualized speech: 'God save the King! Will no man say "Amen"? / Am I both priest and clerk? Well then, Amen. / God save the King, although I be not he' (4.1.173–5). Again, Richard's speech mimics the call-and-response of a liturgy, and he plays both roles, effectively obviating his audience. He taps into the capacity of ritual for social control; as Berger argues, he lays down ground rules that limit the range of possible responses (Berger 54). Here, Richard precludes response, monopolizing a ceremony of his own invention – blessing the un-kinged king – and setting the stage for the invented ritual that defines the play, when he will become both director and subject of the curious last rites of kingship.[16]

As the warder scene demonstrates, rituals often demand physical props, and Richard demands a powerful one before launching a performance that is at once visually provocative and verbally cunning:

> [*to York*] Give me the crown. [*Takes crown.*]
> [*to Bolingbroke*] Here, cousin, seize the crown. Here, cousin.
> On this side my hand on that side thine.
> Now is this golden crown like a deep well
> That owes two buckets, filling one another,
> The emptier ever dancing in the air,
> The other down, unseen and full of water.
> That bucket down, and full of tears, am I,
> Drinking my griefs whilst you mount up on high.
>
> (4.1.181–8)

Berger suggests that these striking lines make Richard complicit in his own demise: 'Whatever we impute to Richard at either the intentional or the motivational level, his actions as well as his language dare Bolingbroke to assume the usurper's role: "Here, cousin, seize the crown"' (Berger 55). However, this is the same man who insists on playing both 'priest and clerk', and he does not relinquish the dual role of usurper/ usurped quite so easily. As Richard's deictic markers show, he retains enough control to divest himself of the crown before Bolingbroke ever gets the chance to 'seize' it. Of particular interest are the demonstrative pronouns *this* and *that*, words that function to distinguish spatial and temporal proximity and distance, respectively (Hope, *Shakespeare's Grammar* 25). Levinson contends that these terms can be exploited to show emotional distance or intimacy in addition to a physical relationship with the speaker: '*this* can mean "the object in a pragmatically given area close to the speaker's location at CT [time of utterance]," and *that* "the object beyond the pragmatically given area close to the speaker's location at CT" ... But the facts are complicated here by the shift from *that* to *this* to show empathy, and from *this* to *that* to show emotional distance (empathetic deixis)' (Levinson 81). Richard uses *this* and *that* to narrate a discomfiting visual display, the incongruous spectacle of crown shared between two would-be kings: 'Here, cousin. On this side my hand and on that side thine.' The deictic demonstratives align Richard with the crown; he marks it as proximal to himself, and emphasizes that Bolingbroke is distanced. The repeated, spondaic 'Here, cousin' reinforces the proximity, since the deictic adverb *here* also indicates physical or emotional closeness. The meaning of 'here', as is the case with many deictic terms, is also bound up with the physical body in the form of gesture. When a speaker thrusts an object towards an interlocutor with the word 'here', the implication is the relinquishment of that object. Yet the proximal connotations of 'here' can mark that act of giving as a reluctant, or even coerced, renunciation. Richard stresses that the crown is part of him, and Bolingbroke will have to violate that relationship of affinity if he is to take it.[17] But a few lines later, in his analogy of the crown as a well, Richard shifts his alliance: 'That bucket down, and full of tears, am I.' The shift to the distal *that*, used with the personal pronoun *I*, represents a relinquishment in Richard prior to any action on Bolingbroke's part. It is a moving statement of his disrupted subject position, and it represents the moment of disconnection. He first aligns himself with the crown and marks it proximally, but we observe every painful detail as he transfers its ownership (note the insistent present tense of the transformative moment, when the crown is still marked proximally but on the cusp of changing hands: '*Now* is this golden crown like a deep well'). His subsequent use of *that* confirms the crown's release, offering an active method of distancing himself and ensuring that it is Bolingbroke who has proximal claims on it. When Richard finally hands over the crown – 'I give this heavy weight from off my head' (203) – it is no longer the crown itself but its 'weight', a burden of both its 'cares' and its absence, that Richard marks as proximal.

Richard's endeavour to redefine ritual so that he may be both priest and clerk, agent and victim, continues with the careful rote progress of an invented ceremony:

BOLINGBROKE
   Are you contented to resign the crown?

RICHARD
   Aye, no. No, aye; for I must nothing be,
   Therefore, no 'no', for I resign to thee.
   Now mark me how I will undo myself:
   I give this heavy weight from off my head,
      [*Gives crown to Bolingbroke.*]
   And this unwieldy sceptre from my hand,
      [*Takes up sceptre and gives it to Bolingbroke.*]
   The pride of kingly sway from out my heart;
   With mine own tears I wash away my balm,
   With mine own hands I give away my crown,
   With mine own tongue deny my sacred state,
   With mine own breath release all duteous oaths.
                                                    (4.1.200–10)

In his deliberate undermining of what he understands to be a 'sacred state', Richard inscribes betrayal and even sacrilege into his invented ritual.[18] The self-cancelling aural effect of 'Aye, no. No; aye' suggests that the in-between identity that Richard has been moving towards is now fully operative; he contends that, without the crown, he 'must nothing be'. Yet the rest of the speech belies this impression, for his controlling voice directs the proceedings. 'Now mark me how I will undo myself,' with its triple self-reference, places an exaggerated emphasis on Richard's agentive role. His modal phase 'I will' (the only instance of the uncontracted *I will* construction by Richard in the play) suggests his complicity and indeed his desire to direct the proceedings. It is a defiant reaction against the dictating *must*, which represents a source of control and action independent of Richard. If he 'must' be nothing, then at the very least he 'will' replace the force behind this imposition with his own power. Richard also exploits the potential for ritualized action to place himself in the spotlight through the continual monitoring and narration of action that positions the speaker as central in the context of ritual. This type of self-orientation 'is part of what it means to occupy a position in the ritual context' (Hanks, *Intertexts* 232). Moreover, these successive descriptions of action ('I give this heavy weight from off my head'; 'With mine own tears I wash away my balm'), that illustrate the type of deictic usage through which 'inhabitants monitor and qualify the linkage between what they are saying and the contexts in which they are doing so' (*Intertexts* 62) establish the speaker's agency, volition and also their intentions for the future. As Hanks asserts, the discourse of ritual is 'marked by frequent use of conventional expressions describing what the performer is doing ... and all these formulae index *intentional* states' (232; emphasis added). The change in tense, and the progression of the verbs, is instructive; after acknowledging the necessary confinement of the present moment – 'I must nothing be', Richard 'resigns', and then moves to reclaim control and volition over the immediate future: 'Now, mark me how I will undo myself.' The next lines suggest the cleansing and relinquishment typical of ritual – 'wash', 'give', 'deny', 'release'[19] – and each statement is marked with a surplus of personal deictic markers: 'With *mine own* tears *I* wash away *my* balm.' The withheld 'I' of the earlier scene in which Richard insisted that 'the king shall do it' here emerges with an almost exaggerated flourish. Richard is no longer hiding, but assuming full agentive responsibility. He inhabits the speaking 'I' role with the most assertive stance that we have seen from him in the entire play.

Richard's new sense of agency sparks a renewed attempt at public control. When Northumberland, angry at Richard's refusal to read aloud the crimes of which he is accused, protests that 'The commons will not then be satisfied' (4.1.272), Richard's reply is resoundingly authoritative: 'They shall be satisfied' (4.1.273). His response, dependent on an authority that has been revoked, seems a reversion to outdated patterns of speech, an appeal to the prerogative of the king to mandate the 'will' of others. Immediately following this presumptuous show of power, Richard returns to his familiar role of regaining control through re-referencing in an action that strongly recalls the warder scene. After demanding a looking glass, Richard gazes on his face and claims to reject its 'brittle glory' (4.1.287): 'Was this face the face / That every day under his household roof / Did keep ten thousand men? Was this the face / That like the sun did make beholders wink?' (4.1.281–4). The use of *this* in these lines, a repeated indicator of proximity, initially establishes a contiguous relationship between his face and his identity.[20]

However, this proximity begins to recede as Richard shifts to the neutral 'As brittle as the glory is *the* face' (287), pushing the image of the face away from himself (by using *the*, he marks the face as in-between, neither proximal nor distal). Then, in a grand theatrical gesture, he smashes the mirror and cements the distal relationship, saying, 'For *there* it is, cracked in a hundred shivers' (288). In one sense, by moving neatly from the proximal *this* to the distal *there*, this passage acts as a virtual chart of Richard's rejection of 'the king' who 'must' submit to the mandates of others, now reduced to '*that* face', broken on the floor. On the field at Coventry, the thrown warder represented an expansion of the deictic centre, a means by which Richard might extend his influence. Here, the act of corporeal expansion is reinforced by the polysemy charted by Richard's deictic markers. Even as he claims to relinquish his old face, he clings to it. His final reference to the face is deictically proximal and proprietary – '*my* face' (4.1.291) – and the very act of throwing the mirror, a kingly gesture reminiscent of his strongest show of power in the play, shows him seeking to retain his claim on all subject positions: the king, the man behind the title, and the curious in-between role of one 'greater than a king' (4.1.305). Curiously, this mirror scene suggests a greater strength at Richard's disposal than that available to him in the warder scene. The difference is in the multiple positions that converge so readily: here he inhabits the role of 'unkinged' Richard as fearlessly as he once occupied the position of 'king'.

Elam suggests that much of the progression of a dramatic text may be traced to a succession of various 'deictic orientations'; different characters take turns inhabiting the central speaking *I* role, addressing various *you*s, thereby creating a clearly segmented sequence. This sequence may be further subdivided by the changes in orientation undergone by individual characters: 'each time the speaker changes indexical direction, addresses a new "you", indicates a different object, enters into a different relationship with his situation or his fellows, a new semiotic unit is set up' (Elam 145). Despite its anchoring function, deixis also reflects fluctuation: conditions are always changing, and as a result new situations are always being initiated. Deixis, then, is a useful way to linguistically map the fluctuations of the speaking subject; the speaker is always engaged in self-situating, but, as Richard's position in this play conspicuously illustrates, the relationship between speaker and situation is never fixed. Given that the common words of deixis work to orient the self, what we find by tracking these markers is a window into the speaker's inner world. Richard's deictic orientation inscribes how he conceives of himself, how he endeavours to protect himself, and the means by which he actively constitutes himself as a subject in the world. His variable deictic markers show him re-making the boundary between himself and the world, changing his own position in response to the shifting ground beneath him.

Like modality, deixis linguistically represents a site of contact between the self and the world, and it may be understood in similar terms as a crucial indicator of the struggle taking place on that border: 'It is a central means of contestation, and the site of working out, whether by negotiation or imposition, of ideological systems' (Hodge and Kress 123). King Richard consistently attempts to reposition himself in relation to the world, to find a new centre, and with his 'own tongue' to create a threshold between identities that somehow bypasses the traditional conflict zone of self and other. Richard strives to find the loopholes in his language, while at the same time he ruminates on the implications of his manipulation: as Brian Cummings observes, 'at the same time as trying to do these complex things in language he also attempts to investigate the very processes by which language does these things' (*Mortal Thoughts* 186). We see this tendency in the language of the deposition scene, and it is also evident at the end of the play when Richard is proximal to no one but himself: 'I have been studying how I may compare / This prison where I live unto the world; / And for because the world is populous, / And *here* is not a creature but myself, / I cannot do it. Yet I'll hammer't out' (5.5.1–5; emphasis added). In these final moments, Richard's declaration of inability is superseded by his volitional agency. The tension between these forces – the dictates of a world that determines what he 'cannot' do, and the desire to reclaim control – are inscribed in the small words by which Richard identifies himself and his place in the world.

4

As You Like It: 'Much virtue in "if"'

In *As You Like It* the experience – or lack – of formal schooling provides a vital subtext. The play opens with a complaint from a thwarted scholar. Orlando's first words lament the contrast between his position and that of his middle brother at the hands of their callous eldest brother Oliver: 'My brother Jaques he keeps at school and report speaks goldenly of his profit. For my part, he keeps me rustically at home or, to speak more properly, stays me here at home unkept' (1.1.4–7). The sting in this injustice seems to derive from a number of sources. Orlando's 'rustic' home life and his lack of education are made even less tolerable by the evident gains enjoyed by Jaques. The rewards of Jaques's education are figured in terms of wealth, in the 'golden' report of his 'profit', and they serve to accent Orlando's impoverished state. Orlando also appears to have a scholar's discerning ear for the subtleties of language use; even unschooled, he vows to 'speak more properly' and substitutes the bland 'keeps' with the evocative (and atypically transitive) verb 'stays', while cleverly invoking the parallel adjective 'unkept'. In Orlando's keen assessment, speaking 'more properly' means dispensing with pompous Latinate words such as 'rustically' and turning to simpler Saxon terms: 'stays me here at home'. Later in the scene, the villainous Oliver privately admits that his brother is 'never schooled and yet learned' (1.1.156), an observation borne out when Orlando composes his verses. While his skill as a poet is questionable, Orlando's familiarity with Ovid and other classical influences is apparent: 'Nature presently distilled / Helen's cheek but not her heart, / Cleopatra's majesty, / Atalanta's better part, / Sad Lucretia's modesty' (3.2.141–5).

An appreciation of the rewards of learning and a concomitant understanding of the costs of being excluded (as well as the virtue of seeking out alternative forms of education) permeates the dramatic world of *As You Like It*. Grammar school makes a memorable cameo in the play's most quoted passage, Jaques's vivid characterization of the seven ages: 'At first the infant, / Mewling and puking in the nurse's arms; / Then the whining schoolboy with his satchel / And shining morning face, creeping like snail / Unwillingly to school' (2.7.144–8). The griping and the heel-dragging attest to a universal sort of revulsion. Jaques's grasp of children's sour opinion of school may be rooted not merely in his attentiveness to human psychology, but also in a formative memory. William Lily's *Shorte Introduction of Grammar* (first published in 1540), the ubiquitous textbook of the Tudor grammar school and a shared cultural touchstone that moulded early understandings of language and education, offered another sort of 'common language' for Shakespeare and his contemporaries. Jaques's representation of the reluctant schoolboy echoes a familiar passage in Lily's *Grammar*. The standard edition of the Introduction to the *Grammar* concluded with a work called *Carmen de moribus*, or 'poem on morals' (after Cato's work of the same name). Lily's *Carmen* is a poem only in the loosest sense; while it is arranged in elegiac metre, it reads more like a rulebook for schoolboys than a work of literature. Nevertheless, it has been useful to critics as a glimpse into the expectations held by English schoolmasters for conduct in their classrooms, and it represents the first example of written literature that most Elizabethan children – including Shakespeare – would have encountered: '*Carmen de moribus* was a well-known text used in the most influential schools in the country ... Apart from textbooks on grammar, it has often been printed with other pedagogical works, but as a result of being incorporated into the English part of the authorized grammar it gained general currency and has been memorized by many generations of schoolchildren' (Gwosdek 81). The first lines of the *Carmen de moribus* offer a step-by-step guide for preparing for school in the morning:

> Qui mihi discipulus puer es, cupis atque doceri, Huc ades, haec animo concipe dicta tuo. Mane situs lectum fuge, mollem discute somnum: Templa petas supplex, et uenerare deum. Attamen in primis facies sit lota, manus'que, Sint nitidae uestes, compta'que caesaries. Desidiam fugiens, cum te schola nostra uocarit Adsis, nulla pigre sit tibi causa morae. (Child who are my scholar, and you desire to be taught, come here, grasp firmly these sayings in your mind. Early in the morning leave your bed, shake off gentle sleep. Humbly go into the church, and worship God. But first of all, let your face be washed and your hands, let your garments be clean and your hair combed. Avoid idleness when our school calls you. Have no excuse for lazy dawdling.) (Gwosdek 204–5)

The 'shining morning face' of Jaques's representative schoolboy attests to his success in performing the morning ablutions prescribed in the poem. *Carmen*'s admonition against idleness is not so easily satisfied, however, with 'lazy dawdling' (also rendered as 'sluggish delay' in some translations[1]) captured in Jaques's evocative phrase 'creeping like snail'. This allusion is the sort that is easily lost as common cultural reference points fall away. Yet for a considerable component of Shakespeare's first audiences, encounters with Lily's *Grammar* were synonymous with the earliest memories of schooling.

The topic of Shakespeare's grammar has little of the panache of other language-related subjects like wordplay and rhetoric, suggestive instead, perhaps, of a dreary didacticism. While the discussion in this chapter stops short of making claims for grammar's misunderstood elegance, it does ask us to think seriously about the ways in which early modern understandings of grammar differ from our own. Today, 'grammar' tends to have a fairly rigid set of associations, and these are most often linked to proper usage. Notions of precision, acceptability and convention (of *rules*, in other words) are what form the basis of our typical ideas about grammar; no wonder we tend to find it boring. In early modern England, however – indeed, in early modern Europe at large – grammar was a more capacious category: it could refer to an array of practices, from the study of Latin, the vernacular, or foreign languages; to translation, etymology and language use in general.

In this chapter, I am taking a broad view of grammar, considering at once its significant history as a humanist cornerstone and pedagogical tool in Tudor classrooms, and its injunctions about the rules of usage for both Latin and English, as exemplified in texts such as Lily's *Grammar* and William Bullokar's *Bref Grammar of English* (1586). The experience of the grammar school itself provides another vital source of 'common' language and experience. In this sense, 'grammar' represents a foundational ideal of humanist education, a means of codifying and structuring a language and offering concrete rules for proper usage. In addition to this institutional notion of grammar, I also draw on the term to refer to linguistic details such as syntax and verb morphology. 'Grammar' constitutes a wide category that encompasses the public face of language, the prescriptive rules of usage, as well as the internal structuring of the language, the grammatical choices that speakers make. This chapter considers two different but related stories of grammar and *As You Like It*: one about the teaching of language, and the ways in which grammar is learned, reinforced and deployed rhetorically, and another about the English language itself, and the ways in which a common word such as *if* opens up a wealth of expressive possibilities.

It is not unusual for the term 'grammar', one of the most ambiguous categories in the lexicon of linguistics, to cover such broad ground.[2] In early modern England, grammar was an elastic concept, subject to 'riotous diversity' in its definitions, and used to refer to everything from the study of Latin, the vernacular, or foreign languages, to translation, etymology, language use, and the language itself. Indeed, there is a strong correlation between linguistic change and innovation and debates about grammar, and because the early modern period featured such remarkable linguistic change, the age was characterized by 'numerous conflicts over what is called "grammar"' (Mitchell 1–2). Disputes were fed, in part, by changing perceptions about Latin and English, for in the late sixteenth century, English was only just beginning to be thought of as a language that had a structure, order and grammar of its own. In its broader sense, too, 'grammar' in early modern England held a more prominent place in literary culture than in its present-day incarnations. From the Middle Ages, *grammatica* was at the heart of literacy and learning, the foundational practice that 'underpins all intellectual activity in the Renaissance' (Hope, *Shakespeare and Language* 34). *Grammatica* was the first part of the *trivium*, followed by logic (*dialectica*) and rhetoric (*rhetorica*), and together these disciplines comprised the three essential components of medieval education, and subsequently formed the cornerstones of humanist pedagogy. However, grammar alone transcended the role of mere scholarly discipline. As Brian Cummings explains, the scope and influence of grammar in the Middle Ages was wide; it 'was the *ars* before and within every other *ars*', a concept that 'covered the full range of the linguistic and the literary, the semantics and the semiotic'. This legacy persisted into the early modern period, as 'grammar continued to encompass not only the acquisition of basic language skills and the engendering of literary "eloquence," but also the interpretation of linguistic meaning or of literary theory' (*Literary Culture* 21–2). In short, in the period concurrent with Shakespeare's lifetime, 'grammar' could be associated with language in all of its guises. In this unusually rich and dynamic linguistic age, the term could effectively refer to any aspect of language use, including writing, speaking, learning and analysis.[3] Early modern writers such as Shakespeare, who traded in the currency of words, had good reason to be attuned to the various aspects of grammar, for they defined the parameters for eloquence, play and possibility within their language. Shakespeare's grammar, broadly conceived, suggests the ways in which he was attuned to circulating ideas about language, as well as to the expressive possibilities created by the distinctive linguistic climate of his age.

One key element that I am placing in the generous category of 'Shakespeare's grammar' is the influence of the Tudor grammar school. In the period in which Shakespeare came of age, grammar school cast a long cultural shadow. It was both the remembered site of control and discipline for generations of English citizens and a touchstone for more pervasive arenas such as social mobility, class and politics. The push for humanist education meant that grammar schools proliferated in sixteenth-century England, and while different schools unmistakably offered diverse experiences – the King's Free Grammar School in Stratford, which Shakespeare presumably attended, was much smaller and more provincial than famous London schools like St Paul's and Merchant Taylor's[4] – one important similarity was their royally mandated textbook, Lily's *Grammar*. English schoolboys, unlike their Continental counterparts, were united by a common book; the 1540 edition prescribes the exclusive use of this work for the teaching of grammar with the edict 'ut non alia quam haec una per totam Angliam pueris praelegeretur' (Gwosdek 8). In short, all of the teaching and learning of Latin in England was to be mediated through this single book and the use of any alternative was effectively illegal. As Leah Whittington observes, 'from its earliest printing under Henry VIII, the "Royal Grammar" came accompanied by grand pronouncement of universal reach and authority' (87).[5] The Royal Grammar, so fundamental in shaping formative perspectives on language, became a shared cultural reference: 'not only did it set down the "correct text," but comprised a great part of the children's personal learning and defined their modes of thought' (Gwosdek 1). This work, together with the *Book of Common Prayer*, also imposed by royal proclamation, formed an essential component of the intellectual and moral development of generations of citizens in early modern England. Shakespeare could rely on this common grounding in a significant part of his audience – who could be expected to groan in recognition at the appearance of or reference to a punishing teacher or a tedious textbook onstage – just as he shared with many of them the habits of mind shaped by their shared grammar school experience.

Middle-class boys in sixteenth-century England typically began their grammar school education at age seven, and spent each day of their early years in the classroom engaged in long hours of rote memorization and drills in the basics of Latin grammar (Potter 116).[6] Such an environment promoted a rapid entrée into adulthood, as schoolboys were taught to surrender 'the simple, sensual pleasures of early childhood' in favour of the virtues of renunciation and restraint (Lamb, 'Apologizing for Pleasure' 505). In the transition from childhood nursery to regimented classroom, pupils were swiftly inculcated into the virtues of order and obedience, subject to the paternal control and magisterial authority of the schoolmaster (Enterline 38).[7] In *Shakespeare's Schoolroom*, Lynn Enterline describes how the structure and ethos of Tudor grammar school classrooms contoured the practice of writing and the literary and critical works that emerged in late sixteenth-century England. It is not simply training in Latin grammar that was significant to English writers such as Shakespeare; the repeated emphasis on performance, punishment and an embodied and often eroticized relationship to rhetoric and grammar also left an unmistakable mark on Elizabethan literature. Of course, the interrogation of the relationship between grammar school discipline and nascent eroticism is not new: Walter Ong long ago observed that grammar school training was a prominent male puberty rite in which seemingly ceaseless grammar drills disciplined the body as well as the mind. Yet Enterline both returns to and expands these foundational ideas. The 'theatricality of everyday life', to borrow one of her resonant characterizations, and the emphasis on regular public performance as part of the grammar school curriculum, is a useful way to help collapse the longstanding, anachronistic division between rhetoric and drama. Additionally, Enterline suggests that because imitation was the backbone of humanist pedagogy, and because it was so closely linked to impersonation in the school's everyday life, one notable consequence of humanist training was to reveal that familiar roles – such as 'a boy', 'a woman', 'a father' (all of which commonly appeared in school textbooks) – might in fact be socially scripted parts. In undercutting these categories, and in creating character effects of emotion and subjectivity, Shakespeare subtly displays the formative effects of his grammar school training.

Shakespeare's most prominent homage to his formative schooling may be found in his 'monument to the problems of grammar and rhetoric', *Love's Labour's Lost* (Barkan 38). The characters of *Love's Labour's Lost* are emblematic of various apparent linguistic ills. The speech of Don Armado drowns in inkhornisms, and that of the curate Nathaniel is nearly wholly reliant on formulaic aphorisms. Holofernes, meanwhile, provides Shakespeare's most cutting caricature of a schoolmaster, one whose excessive Latinisms reveal him as a braggart and a blowhard: 'Yet a kind of insinuation, as it were, *in via*, in way, of explication, *facere*, as it were, replication, or rather *ostentare*, to show, as it were, his inclination' (4.2.12–14). Here, actual Latin terms are interspersed with Latin-derived words to amusing effect; far from the elucidating quality that one would wish from a teacher, Holofernes's words muddy interpretation. Overt schoolmaster types in Shakespeare tend to be authoritarian or buffoonish – and often both. Even plays with less apparent emphasis on the rituals and outcomes of the classroom than *Love's Labour's Lost* present memorable scenes of instruction. *The Merry Wives of Windsor* features a garbled grammar lesson delivered by Sir Hugh Evans in which the declension of Latin verbs devolves into nonsense and double entendre:

EVANS
What is he, William, that does lend articles?

WILLIAM
Articles are borrowed of the pronoun, and be thus declined. *Singulariter* nominativo: 'hic, haec, hoc.'

EVANS
Nominativo: hig, hag, hog. Pray you mark: *genitivo:* '*huius.*' Well, what is your accusative case?

WILLIAM
Accusativo: 'hinc' –

EVANS
I pray you have your remembrance, child. *Accustivo:* '*hing, hang, hog.*'

MISTRESS QUICKLY
'Hang-hog' is Latin for bacon, I warrant you.

(4.1.32–41)

Sir Hugh's attempts at pedagogical decorum are undercut by the peculiarities of his Welsh accent, just as Mistress Quickly's sharp ear for slang overshadows any concern for William's performance. The enactment of instruction on Shakespeare's stage tends to follow the trajectory from earnest mimicry to mayhem demonstrated in *Merry Wives*; the music lesson in *The Taming of the Shrew* and the French-English lesson in *Henry V* are similarly awash with puns and jests.

Other Shakespearean references to the grammar school experience gesture towards that common experience of so many English schoolboys. In *Much Ado About Nothing*, Benedick quotes a passage from Lily's *Grammar*, just as in *Titus Andronicus* Chiron recognizes 'a verse in Horace, I know it well. / I read it in the grammar long ago' (4.2.23–4). Aaron's response to Chiron exposes the problem in his claim:

Ay, just, a verse in Horace; right, you have it
[*Aside*] Now what a thing it is to be an ass!
Here's no sound jest. The old man hath found their guilt,
And sends them weapons wrapped about with lines
That wound beyond their feeling to the quick.

(4.2.25–9)

Whittington observes that Chiron's 'Latin studies have evidently done him little good. He recognizes the provenance of the lines, but entirely misses their relevance to his own situation' (88). This passage, in its sketch of a mediocre pupil, exemplifies the dominant flavour of school-related allusions in Shakespeare: ironic, acerbic and sceptical. In Shakespeare's works, 'remembrance[s]' of the classroom, to use Sir Hugh's term, are marbled with pompous authority and hollow teachings. When Tranio, in *The Taming of the Shrew*, asks Gremio if he has just returned from church, Gremio's sardonic response is 'As willingly as I e'er came from school' (3.2.149); in other words, most willingly. Prospero is recognizably demanding in the mould of both a father and a pedagogue, with 'a grammar school master's penchant for instructing (and dominating) his pupils' (Enterline 174). The Duke of Gloucester in *Henry VI, Part 1* draws on the weakness of impressionable students to deride Winchester: 'None do you like but an effeminate prince, / Whom, like a school-boy, you may over-awe' (1.1.37). Even Shakespeare's sonnet speaker occasionally assumes the persona of a timid scholar, his 'pupil pen' (16.10) suggestive of youthful insecurity and ineptitude. Elsewhere, the sonnet speaker points to the illumination of a reluctantly learned lesson – 'But thence I learn, and find the lesson true' (118.13) – to demonstrate the hard-won virtues of learning, an idea which is supported by the repeated warnings of the perils of being 'untutored' and 'unlearned' (138.3, 4).

In keeping with other references to schooling in Shakespeare, which tend to satirize and expose the deficiencies of the sanctioned schoolroom, *As You Like It* emphasizes non-standard channels of learning. In a memorable characterization, Duke Senior points to the isolation and pastoral comfort of the Forest of Arden as an alternative source of education for his court-accustomed cohort: 'And this our life, exempt from public haunt / Finds tongues in trees, books in the running brooks, / Sermons in stones, and good in everything' (2.1.16–18). Nature as teacher is a longstanding cliché of the pastoral mode. In Duke Senior's assessment, though, the often-vexing tools of the grammar school – the ancient 'tongues' that pupils were required to learn, the standard 'books' that demanded daily study – are here transformed into items of delight. They are not foisted upon students, but rather 'found' or discovered as a part of daily life in the forest. Amiens praises Duke Senior's words using the terms of a grammar school student accustomed to monitoring and assessing the academic performance of himself and his classmates: 'I would not change it. Happy is your grace / That can translate the stubbornness of fortune / Into so quiet and sweet a style' (2.1.18–20).[8] Amiens means that Duke Senior is good at finding the silver lining in misfortune, yet he is also following the Duke's lead in transforming the oppressive conditions of grammar school into sources of liberation. Just as the burdensome 'books' of the schoolroom are in the forest changed to enchanting 'brooks', the skill of 'translat[ion]' so central to the grammar school model becomes a sort of alchemy by which the stubborn is made sweet. The 'style' of the forest, this exchange suggests, could not be more different from that of the classroom. Of course, there are limits to the idealized sphere of nature's schoolroom. Immediately following this exchange, the bliss is punctured by a Lord's florid description of a dying stag, whose 'big round tears / Coursed one another down his innocent nose / In piteous chase' (2.1.38–40). According to the Lord, the pitiful scene prompts Jaques to 'moralize th[e] spectacle', as any well-trained scholar would, 'into a thousand similes' (2.1.44–5). With this report, the lessons of nature have veered into the ridiculous, with Jaques 'weeping and commenting / Upon the sobbing deer' (2.1.65–6).

This scene offers a nutshell summary of the treatment of pedagogy in *As You Like It*. Associations of learning are set askew; distorted and satirical invocations of grammar school are contrasted with other modes of instruction that are alternately inspired and absurd. Touchstone is emblematic of the play's double-edged perspective on schooling. His fool's wisdom owes a great deal to recognizable patterns of formal instruction, but it also retains a concrete footing in farce. Touchstone is conversant in the discourse of grammar, yet his allusions tend to be off-centre in a manner that befits his 'motley' disposition, as when he refers to the courting couples as 'country copulatives' (5.4.55). In his discussion with Corin about the relative merits of a shepherd's life, Touchstone demonstrates the prized ability to consider both sides of a question with equal dedication:

> Truly, shepherd, in respect of itself, it is a good life; but in respect that it is a shepherd's life, it is naught. In respect that it is solitary, I like it very well; but in respect that it is private, it is a very vile life. Now in respect it is in the fields, it pleaseth me well; but in respect it is not in the court, it is tedious. As it is a spare life, look you, it fits my humour well; but as there is no more plenty in it, it goes much against my stomach. (3.2.13–20)

Touchstone here practices an extreme form of *quaestio*, the rhetorical exercise of deliberation on either side of a question that was instilled in all grammar school boys in Shakespeare's England. This skill, foundational to humanist practice and pedagogy, transcended the classroom to become a sort of trained habit. Joel Altman has called the practice of arguing both sides of a question 'the moral cultivation of ambivalence', and suggests that it flourished not only in discussions of politics, philosophy, theology and the like, but also 'simply as a creative pastime' (32). In other words, a good round of *quaestio* could serve as an amusing and satisfying diversion.

Shakespeare's formative lessons in considering both sides of the question find an echo in his works: 'repeatedly he transfers those skills to characters within his plays and poems in ways that wryly recognize both the fascination of those methods and their potential for sicklying o'er the name of action with a pale cast of words' (Burrow 17). In Touchstone's case, unlike Hamlet's, it is not that copious words and debate stand in for action; rather, his *quaestio* becomes an exercise in self-cancelling. When something is determined to be both pleasing and tedious, amenable and foul, the debate is all but lost. Or is it? Beneath the absurdity of Touchstone's opposing conclusions are shades of nuance borne out in the play. Duke Senior and his lords might agree that there is a meaningful difference between a solitary life and a private life, and that existence apart from the court offers rewards and tedium in equal measure. Orlando's confessed surprise and self-correction when encountering the lords in the forest – 'I thought that all things had been savage here' (2.7.107) – reinforces the spirit of Touchstone's rhetorical exercise. Later in his debate with the 'natural philosopher' Corin, Touchstone demands that assertions directed at the hapless – and, as in *Merry Wives*, tellingly named – William be bolstered with proof – 'Instance, briefly. Come, instance' (3.2.49) – and rejects those that he finds insufficient: 'A better instance, I say' (3.2.54); 'A more sounder instance, come!' (3.2.58). Touchstone's skill in criticism extends beyond academic performance to literary analysis, calling Orlando's dreary poems 'the very false gallop of verses. Why do you infect yourself with them?' (3.2.110–11). At other points in the play, as well, Touchstone's speech is reminiscent of that of a dogmatic, if erratic, schoolmaster. His most vicious lesson is directed at the unfortunate William:

TOUCHSTONE
Give me your hand. Art thou learned?

WILLIAM
No, sir.

TOUCHSTONE
> Then learn this of me: to have is to have. For it is a figure in rhetoric that drink, being poured out of a cup into a glass, by filling the one doth empty the other. For all your writers do consent that *ipse* is 'he.' Now you are not *ipse*, for I am he.

WILLIAM
> Which he, sir?

TOUCHSTONE
> He, sir, that must marry this woman. Therefore, you clown, abandon (which is, in the vulgar, 'leave') the society (which in the boorish is 'company') of this female (which in the common is 'woman').

(5.1.38–50)

Touchstone cloaks the obvious in pseudo-profound terms borrowed from (dubious) logic. He doesn't need Latin and rhetoric to make his point, and his translations of Latinate terms to the 'vulgar', 'boorish', and 'common' are laughably facile and redundant. Like the melancholy Jaques crying and declaiming on the dying stag, Touchstone here pushes the figure of the scholar well into the realm of caricature. Yet, as ever, his fool's insight is keen, and the lesson's absurdity masks a kernel or two of wisdom, just as it earns him success. Touchstone 'has rigged the arrangement so that William has to give him the answer he is looking for – a technique stolen from Socrates' (Kuhn 44).[9] His pedagogical performance, flawed as it is, nevertheless cements Touchstone's role as autocratic schoolmaster, down to the promise of beating: 'make thee away, translate thy life into death, thy liberty into bondage. I will deal in poison with thee, or in bastinado or in steel. I will bandy with thee in faction; I will o'errun thee with policy. I will kill thee a hundred and fifty ways! Therefore tremble and depart' (5.1.52–7).

If Touchstone is, fittingly, both the play's strict pedant and class clown, then Rosalind is its resident schoolmaster-mistress. She firmly rejects the role of pupil, even in jest: 'Unless you could teach me to forget a banished father, you must not learn me how to remember any extraordinary pleasure' (1.2.5–7). 'Learn' could be a transitive verb in early modern English, and 'learn me' an acknowledgement of or appeal to wisdom, a variant of 'teach me' that places an accent on the subject's *acquisition* – of learning, of grace, of wisdom. Rosalind shrinks from the act of acquiring knowledge in favour of dispensing it, preferring instead the position of sage teacher, as when she offers to tutor Orlando in the ways of love: 'Yet I profess curing it by counsel' (3.2.388). As Ganymede, fending off queries from Orlando about her courtly accent, Rosalind figures her role as teacher as a sort of family inheritance:

> But indeed, an old religious uncle of mine taught me to speak, who was in his youth an inland man – one that knew courtship too well, for there he fell in love. I have heard him read many lectures against it and I thank God I am not a woman, to be touched with so many giddy offences as he hath generally taxed their whole sex withal. (3.2.331–8)

Ganymede places his role as a scholar firmly in the past, a time-out-of-mind era when he absorbed the lessons of his uncle's lectures against love. In addition to the audience-pleasing irony of 'I thank God I am not a woman,' there is a sly escape-hatch built in to Rosalind/Ganymede's self-appointed role as pedagogue; through Ganymede, Rosalind is liberated from a woman's 'giddy offences' as well as the burden of 'women's gentle brain' (4.3.33–4). Ganymede extends his teacherly role to that of literary evaluator in his critique of Phoebe's letter: 'Why, 'tis a boisterous and a cruel style – / A style for challengers … Women's gentle brain / Could not drop forth such giant, rude invention' (4.3.31–4). Here, Ganymede combines the stern critique of a schoolmaster with an amusingly underhanded challenge to assumptions about who may claim the schoolboy's privilege of rhetorical power. In addition to his role as teacher, Ganymede's authority derives in part from his fluency in the language of the grammar school. Indeed, the figure of Ganymede himself was first introduced to Elizabethan schoolboys in their early translations of Ovid.[10] Heather James has suggested that Shakespeare's female comic heroines use Ovid as a means of taking 'expressive liberties ... with erotic, rhetorical, and social conventions' (68). In her adopted persona, Rosalind creates a figure who is recognizably Ovidian and wonderfully liberating: 'Putting on "doublet and hose" and the name Ganymede, Rosalind throws herself into the world of erotic games and theatre delineated in Ovid's early poems, the *Ars Amatoria* and *Amores* in which love and poetry alike are games and toys' (James 74).

Both in and out of her Ganymede persona, Rosalind is skilled in the mainstays of the Tudor grammar school curriculum. Again, Lily's *Grammar* provides an intriguing intertext. In addition to its literary status as a rudimentary poem, the textbook's *Carmen de moribus* also offers an introductory reading list for grammar school pupils:

> Grammaticas, recte si vis cognoscere, leges: Discere si cupias cultius ore loqui, Addiscas veterum, clarissima scripta, virorum, Et quos autores, turba latina, docet. Nunc te Vergilius, nunc ipse Terentius optat: Nunc simul amplecti te Ciceronis opus. Quos qui non didicit, nil praeter somnia vidit: Certat & in tenebris vivere Cimmeriis.
> (If you wish to correctly know the laws of grammar, if you desire to speak more elegantly, learn the most famous writings of the old and which authors the Latin crowd suggests. Now Virgil picks you out, now Terence himself, now at the same time the work of the esteemed Cicero picks you out. He who has not learned these, he sees nothing but dreams, and he struggles to live in Cimmerian darkness.)

The classical authors recommended as models of elegant speech provided the foundations of Shakespeare's education in language and literature. Moreover, these Latin masters are invoked not simply as exemplars but also as personal teachers, capable of bridging the gap between the classical and early modern words to tap English schoolboys on the shoulder and 'pick them out' for tutelage.[11] The emphasis here lies in improbably private and direct relationships, despite gulfs of time and language, between teacher and student, literary predecessor and protégé. Rosalind/Ganymede's witty deployment of classical sources owes something to the type of familiar relationship prescribed by Lily. In the memorable dispute between Ganymede and Orlando about the putatively fatal nature of love, Rosalind/Ganymede lays out classical examples in startlingly intimate and irreverent terms:

> The poor world is almost six thousand years old, and in all this time there was not any man died in his own person (videlicet, in a love-cause). Troilus had his brains dashed out with a Grecian club, yet he did what he could to die before, and he is one of the patterns of love. Leander, he would have lived many a fair year though Hero had turned nun, if it had not been for a hot midsummer night; for, good youth, he went but forth to wash him in the Hellespont and, being taken with the cramp, was drowned, and the foolish chroniclers of that age found it was Hero of Sestos. But these are all lies. Men have died from time to time and worms have eaten them, but not for love. (4.1.86–99)

The expressive impact of this assessment is derived largely from its amusing deflation of courtly love clichés. In Ganymede's revisionist history, classical heroes are just like us: prone to cramps and all too human. Throughout the play Rosalind/Ganymede's invocation of classical models consistently demonstrates this mode of familiarity, their stories told with a sort of eyewitness perspective: 'There was never anything so sudden but the fight of two rams and Caesar's thrasonical brag of "I came, saw, and overcame"' (5.2.28–31). Here, the colourful descriptor 'thrasonical' springs from Thraso, a braggart soldier from Terence's *Eunuchus*. The adjective, while not Shakespeare's invention, was introduced to English in the sixteenth century, the type of word that would have been familiar to former grammar school students. Of course, the 'brag' at the heart of this line – Casaer's *veni, vidi, vici* – would have been instantly recognizable to any schoolboy in the early stages of Latin learning. Rosalind/Ganymede's schoolmaster role is in keeping with the play's off-kilter nature; in the paradoxically civilized wilderness of Arden, with a hero who skirts the boundary between man and woman, learning and education can spring from unexpected avenues. Even Phoebe, the unschooled shepherdess, can quote Marlowe – '"Who ever loved, that loved not at first sight"' (3.5.82) – just as she possesses an innate awareness of the power of style and rhetoric: 'But what care I for words? Yet words do well / When he that speaks them pleases those that hear' (3.5.112–14).

Analyses in earlier chapters of this book have considered moments when Shakespeare's characters call attention, implicitly or explicitly, to unremarkable common words. Coriolanus's angry discourse on the 'shall' of the tribunes, Gaunt's lament for 'this' England and Richard's sly claims on 'this' crown, as well as *Troilus and Cressida*'s subtle consideration of 'will', each highlight moments when Shakespeare invites his readers and audiences to be close readers, and to consider the expressive force of quotidian words. Even terms that operate as function words (or that border on such usage) play a significant part in shaping ideas about character and action. *As You Like It* also features moments of dialogue when characters comment on or note the implications of small words. In her teasing rejoinder to Rosalind's worry about Orlando's continued affection, Celia rests her argument on the great gulf between past and present forms of the verb *to be*:

ROSALIND
   Not true in love?

CELIA
   Yes, when he is in, but I think he is not in.

ROSALIND
You have heard him swear downright he was.

CELIA
'Was' is not 'is'.

(3.4.24–7)

In, was, is: these simple words are the pulse of the exchange. Later in the play, during Touchstone's comically exaggerated lesson in the gradations of polite discourse, he draws attention to a small word that those prone to diplomacy may find especially useful:

O sir, we quarrel in print, by the book, as you have books for good manners. I will name you the degrees: the first, the retort courteous; the second, the quip modest; the third, the reply churlish; the fourth, the reproof valiant; the fifth, the counter-check quarrelsome; the sixth, the lie with circumstance; the seventh, the lie direct. All these you may avoid but the lie direct, and you may avoid that too with an 'if'. I knew when seven justices could not take up a quarrel, but when the parties were met themselves, one of them thought but of an 'if': as, 'if you said so, then I said so'; and they shook hands and swore brothers. Your 'if' is the only peacemaker; much virtue in 'if'. (5.4.89–101)

Various moments in the play prompt recollections of grammar school and grammar texts. In this passage, Touchstone invites listeners to think about another shared cultural reference point: courtesy books that prescribe accepted social behaviours. He links social grace to grammar itself, the lexical choices and syntax that permit speakers to smooth over the bumps in troublesome linguistic encounters. As he asserts, *if* is a word that holds great possibility. Among Shakespeare's common words, it is perhaps the most slippery and versatile. All of the small words discussed in this book – *shall, will, here, this*, among others – share a propensity for camouflage. They tend to blend into the functional workings of the language, and emerge in their own right only when highlighted in some way. Yet *if* is the most function-oriented of these words; unlike *shall* and *will*, it lacks a core notional meaning, and unlike *this and here*, it is not always dependent on the position of the speaker. *If* is primarily grammatical, a crucial component in the structure of the language that enables expressions of conjecture, conditionality, the hypothetical, the possible, and the wished-for.

Lily's *Grammar* has little to say on the matter of *if*, relegating it to a half-page describing conjunctions with a blanket definition: 'a parte of speech that joyneth words and sentences together'. In present-day English, *if* is a subordinating conjunction that introduces an adverbial clause; that is, the information in the subordinate *if*-clause modifies the meaning of the main clause. *If*, while intuitively understood by speakers, tends to be difficult to pin down in terms of semantic meaning:

> Its bulky, bookish synonyms *provided (that)* and *in case of* have little virtue. Sometimes it is possible to do without if by inverting the word order, as in 'were I (had I been) there ... ', 'should you ever meet him ... ' and so forth, but in most cases, when we want to introduce a conditional clause, we say *if*. (Liberman)

While not as closely linked to speaker perspective and position as modal verbs and deictic terms, *if* nevertheless often reveals something of speaker attitude: 'Recognizing the subordinating function of if, we can treat the conditional clause itself as a modal qualifier, one that affects the interpretation of the mood of the main clause' (James 456). Early modern English *if* featured a similar ambiguity to present-day *if*, with the additional complicating factor of an even wider range of options to express *if*-like sentiments (as illustrated, for example, in the peerless opening line of Andrew Marvell's 'To His Coy Mistress' – 'Had we but world enough, and time').[12] We see *had* to express *if* in *As You Like It* in Rosalind's 'Had I before known this young man his son / I should have given him tears unto entreaties' (1.2.225–6). *An/and* could be used interchangeably with *if*, as when an exasperated Jaques takes leave of the poetically bloviating Orlando: 'Nay then, God b'wi' you an you talk in blank verse' (4.1.28–9).[13] 'Were' in place of *if*, archaic to contemporary ears, was commonplace in Shakespeare, as in Orlando's formulation of alternative family histories in his confrontation with Oliver: 'the same tradition takes not away my blood, were there twenty brothers betwixt us' (1.1.45–6); 'Wert thou not my brother I would not take this hand from thy throat till this other hand had pulled out thy tongue for saying so' (1.1.55–6). In *Henry VI, Part 2*, King Henry uses *shall* to convey an *if* meaning: 'but, shall I speak my conscience, / Our kinsman Gloucester is as innocent ... As is the sucking lamb or harmless dove' (3.1.69–72).[14]

While *if* lacks an easily defined denotative meaning, it brims with connotations of possibility. Its appearance at the beginning of a sentence signals an opening, an invitation to consider possibilities and potential. In Shakespeare's works, *if* functions as a particularly powerful and world-creating word. Shakespeare chooses it to begin plays, as in *Twelfth Night*: 'If music be the food of love, play on' (1.1.1), and scenes, as in *The Tempest*: 'If by your art, dearest father, you have / Put the wild waters in this roar, allay them' (1.2.1).[15] *If* also opens five of Shakespeare's sonnets, including 59: 'If there be nothing new, but that which is' (59.1).

Several scholars have commented on the link between Touchstone's aphorism of compromise and evasion – 'much virtue in "if"' – and the proliferation of the word *if* in *As You Like It*. The play's action depends heavily on the suspension of disbelief, the possibility of multiple hypothetical outcomes, and the conditional truths promised by *if*. In a 1977 article in *Shakespeare Quarterly*, Maura Slattery Kuhn suggests that 'an untypically large number of *If*'s appear in this play, more than any other play by Shakespeare, both in absolute frequency and in relative frequency' (44). Scholars today have the advantage of widely accessible digitized databases of Shakespeare's works, and these tools confirm that *As You Like It*'s 138 *if*s represent nearly the highest concentration of this word in Shakespeare's canon (*Othello* claims the top spot with 139 *if*s).[16] However, as Kuhn's claim implies, conclusions drawn from absolute word counts are limited. As Jonathan Hope and Michael Witmore have noted, 'our understanding of the relationship between the frequency of content words and "meaning" is poor' (194) and in any case readers or audiences are unlikely to notice whether *As You Like It* has more instances of *if* than other plays. The relative number of *if*s in *As You Like It* remains high, just as Rosalind, with twenty-seven instances of *if*, uses the word more than twice as often than do other characters in the play.[17] Additionally, because the word *if* is only one of several ways to express conditionals and hypotheticals in Shakespeare's English, it is not (to borrow a Shakespearean phrase) the be-all and the end-all of *if*-like expressions. The point I want to emphasize here, absolute counts of *if* aside, is that Shakespeare in *As You Like It* holds up the word *if* and its multiple meanings and functions for particular attention. The play highlights this most flexible of common words, both openly (in Touchstone's invitation to consider the 'virtue' in *if*) and subtly (in the various *if*-clauses of the play, particularly during pivotal moments in the action). The *if*s of *As You Like It* comprise an understated type of grammar play, with Shakespeare proffering the word as a suggestive illustration of the significant effects that can be initiated by the smallest grammatical units. *If*, with its special ability to shape-shift, crosses grammatical boundaries in a way that dovetails with the other types of boundary crossing represented in the play. It is a word that folds together logic, philosophy, rhetoric and grammar – a blend well suited to a play where the status of these subjects is always in flux and consistently held up for examination.

In keeping with its elastic properties, *if* functions in a variety of ways in its appearances in the play. When Celia, pulling for Orlando in the wrestling match, says 'If I had a thunderbolt in mine eye I can tell who should down' (1.2.205), *if* communicates a fanciful wish for an alternative world where Celia could, Jupiter-like, intervene to defeat Charles.

Later, when she defends Rosalind against her father's charge of treason, Celia's *if* works both as a retort and an appeal to truth: 'if she be a traitor,/Why, so am I' (1.3.70–1). Touchstone, meanwhile, appears to enjoy nothing more than riddling *if*s and games of logic: 'Why, if thou never wast at court thou never sawst good manners; if thou never sawst good manners then thy manners must be wicked, and wickedness is sin and sin is damnation. Thou art in a parlous state, shepherd' (3.2.38–42). Here, in his teasing of Corin, we see Touchstone basing his conditions on false truth conditions, the flimsy underpinnings on which *if* depends. While *if* is not as firmly linked to context as deictic markers such as *this*, nor to semantic associations as are *will* and *shall*, the word nevertheless has pragmatic effects that reveal something of the stance of the speaker using it, and convey a coded message to the listener. One type of *if*-usage particularly illustrative of pragmatic effect is a 'hedging' conditional clause, which 'reduc[es] the speaker's responsibility for the utterance of the consequent cause' (Tedeschi 10). For example, in the strained exchange between Duke Frederick and Rosalind as he declares her banishment, *if* provides a life raft of defiance in Rosalind's otherwise deferential response:

ROSALIND
    I do beseech your grace,
    Let me the knowledge of my fault bear with me.
    If with myself I hold intelligence,
    Or have acquaintance with mine own desires,
    If that I do not dream, or be not frantic–
    As I do trust I am not – then, dear uncle,
    Never so much as in a thought unborn
    Did I offend your highness.

DUKE FREDERICK
    Thus do all traitors.
    If their purgation did consist in words,
    They are as innocent as grace itself.
    Let it suffice thee that I trust thee not.

(1.3.43–52)

Here, Rosalind's blunt contradiction of her uncle's accusation is bracketed by the conditions of *if*, which appeal to her presumption of self-knowledge and sanity. On the surface, then, Rosalind's words obey the principles of decorum and respect that is expected in her exchanges with the duke. She can plausibly retreat from the responsibility and social penalty incurred by direct contradiction. *If*, in this case, appears to be the 'peacemaker' lauded by Touchstone. Pragmatically, however, Rosalind's use of *if* allows for a strong rebuke: it is an indirect means of disagreement, especially because the condition that it stipulates – that she knows her own mind – is unassailable. As his imperious retort shows, Duke Frederick reads the subtext loud and clear. *If* can also signal another type of defiance, in the form of a challenge. When Touchstone defends his position as a courtier to the lords in Arden, he uses *if* as his appeal: 'If any man doubt that, let him put me to my purgation' (5.4.43). The pragmatic effect here is one of defence and rebuttal, the issuing of a challenge to his prospective detractors.

The gender play for which *As You Like It* is renowned also finds comical expression in the manipulation of *if*. One common function of a conditional *if*-clause is to comment on an 'unreal' situation, as in *I would jump in this puddle if I were a child*. For an adult speaker, while the puddle is a real condition, the status of being a child is not, as the *if*-clause makes clear. This sort of real/unreal formulation makes for plenty of ironic merriment in the play:

TOUCHSTONE
> Stand you both forth now. Stroke your chins and swear by your beards that I am a knave.

CELIA
> By our beards – if we had them – thou art.

TOUCHSTONE
> By my knavery – if I had it – then I were.
> But if you swear by that that is not, you are forsworn.
> (1.2.70–5)

In Celia's and Touchstone's *if*s, the boundary between real and unreal is hopelessly muddied. Celia has no beard, apparently, but the actor playing her might. Touchstone's 'knavery' is not as categorically unreal as his phrasing suggests, as his crafty second *if* suggests. Similarly, Rosalind's closing lines in the Epilogue also depend on the troubling of real and unreal states imposed by the fact of the dramatic world: 'If I were a woman I would kiss as many of you as had beards that pleased me, complexions that liked me and breaths that I defied not' (16–18). In the mouth of Rosalind, a female character playing a male character played by a male actor, *if* is working overtime, and the slippage between the conditions of the 'real' world and the fictive world of the drama is thrown into relief by this small word.

One potential problem in analysing the expressive effect of grammatical function words is the fact of their functionality. It goes without saying that every play by Shakespeare contains many *if*s; it is a standard component of his language. Speakers of English, in the early modern period and today, rely on *if* as a crucial component of expressing conditional, conjectural, and hypothetical ideas. Yet in *As You Like It*, *if* is overdetermined, becoming a watchword that is consistently singled out. This highlighting is most evident in Touchstone's extended tribute to the 'only peacemaker' in grammar, but it is also manifest in moments when *if* is deployed to rhetorical and poetic effect. In instances of *if*-anaphora, readers and audiences are encouraged to pause on this word and its effects:

ORLANDO
   If ever you have looked on better days,
   If ever been where bells have knolled to church,
   If ever sat at any good man's feast,
   If ever from your eyelids wiped a tear,
   And know what 'tis to pity and be pitied –
   Let gentleness my strong enforcement be,
   In the which hope I blush and hide my sword.
                                                      (2.7.114–20)

Orlando's lyricism here is part of his endeavour to win the pity of the lords of Arden, to demonstrate his position as an equal not only through shared human experience but also through a collective memory of life beyond the forest. As in the example of Rosalind and Duke Frederick above, the pragmatic import to Orlando's *if*s is distancing the speaker from the core assertion or request. In Orlando's case, he softens his request for hospitality and 'gentleness' by the appeals of his *if*s. But 'if ever' also transforms into poetic phrase, a cadenced reminder of all that can be invoked by memory of a time before the forest. *As You Like It* asks its readers and audiences to be continuously alert to various forms of poetic language – from songs, to doggerel posted on trees, to the musings of lovesick shepherds and melancholy lords – and *if* becomes a key term in the play's unique lexicon. In Orlando's speech, it is a signal of shared remembrance, while for Silvius, it is a condition that restricts access to a shared experience:

SILVIUS
   O, thou didst never love so heartily!
   If thou rememb'rest not the slightest folly
   That ever love did make thee run into,
   Thou hast not loved.
   Or if thou hast not sat as I do now,
   Wearing thy hearer in thy mistress' praise,
   Thou hast not loved.
   Or if thou hast not broke from company
   Abruptly as my passion now makes me,
   Thou hast not loved.

(2.4.30–9)

Again, *if* becomes part of a poetic refrain, the anticipatory set-up that culminates, repeatedly, in the satisfying rhythm of 'Thou hast not loved.' In Shakespeare's hands, *if* is a potent literary word, its characteristic flexibility and ambiguity allowing for inventive expressive play.

If, with its capacity to invoke imagined, hoped-for, or otherwise unreal worlds, is also exceptionally salient to drama. As Keir Elam has suggested, 'dramatic worlds are hypothetical ("as if") constructs, that is, they are recognized by the audience as counterfactual (i.e. non-real) states of affairs but are embodied as if in progress in the actual here and now' (90). Elam contends that in thinking about a poetics of drama, we must attend to 'the "world-creating" operations of texts and the conceptual labours they call for from their decoders (readers, spectators, etc.)' (90). The stance of readers and audiences towards a drama may be thought of as an *if*-orientation: our vital role is to understand that the dramatic world that we witness unfolding is simultaneously linked to and removed from the 'actual' world. As Robert Shaughnessy observes, '"if" levers the real into the fictive' (40). *As You Like It* is concerned with the mechanics of world creation at a number of different levels: in the alternative world of Arden, the self-fashioning of Ganymede and Aliena, and the meta-commentary on dramatic worlds encouraged in the Epilogue and elsewhere. It is fitting that in this play, where so much hinges on the solace-giving possibility of other worlds and other selves, *if* becomes a byword. Contingencies and possible worlds become 'real' through the workings of *if*: 'Possible – as opposed to actual – states of affairs may be set up through hypothesis, through the expression of wishes ... or through counterfactual conditionals' (Elam 88–9).

The play's resolution hinges on the conditions promised by *if*. Rosalind/Ganymede pushes the truth conditions on which *if* depends, and which Touchstone has primed us to notice, both in his own manipulations of *if*'s truth conditions and in his paean to its 'virtue':

ROSALIND
> [*to* SILVIUS] I will help you if I can. [*to* PHOEBE] I would love you if I could. – Tomorrow meet me all together. [*to* PHOEBE] I will marry you, if ever I marry woman, and I'll be married tomorrow. [*to* ORLANDO] I will satisfy you, if ever I satisfied man, and you shall be married tomorrow. [*to* SILVIUS] I will content you, if what pleases

you contents you, and you shall be married tomorrow.
[*to* ORLANDO] As you love Rosalind, meet. [*to* SILVIUS]
As you love Phoebe, meet. – And as I love no woman,
I'll meet. So fare you well. I have left you commands.

SILVIUS
I'll not fail, if I live.

PHOEBE   Nor I.

ORLANDO   Nor I.

(5.2.106–19)

Ganymede's *if*-conditions, despite their apparent impossibility, are accepted by his audience, who take their 'commands' seriously. Kuhn observes that 'the forest of Arden embodies an unreal condition for the exiles. By accepting its premises, they are rewarded with conclusions transcending their expectations' (49). There is a kind of magic in these *if*s, as the play's characters recognize. And the 'reward' extends to the audience; in this ending, *if* is the catalyst for the delightful formula of Shakespearean comedy. Disbelief is suspended, faith rewarded and reunion realized:

DUKE SENIOR
If there be truth in sight, you are my daughter.

ORLANDO
If there be truth in sight, you are my Rosalind.

PHOEBE
If sight and shape be true,
Why then my love adieu.

ROSALIND
I'll have no father, if you be not he.
I'll have no husband, if you be not he.
Nor ne'er wed woman, if you be not she.

(5.3.116–22)

In *As You Like It, if* showcases its remarkable depths. Its very commonness and functionality augment its shape-shifting, polysemous and ambiguous properties. Even in a play with conventionally lyrical phrases and often-quoted lines, *if* emerges as a potent and poetic word, emblematic of the unexpectedly resonant and expressive 'common' language that Shakespeare so skilfully engaged.

Part of my endeavour in this book has been to work towards a new appreciation of the small details of Shakespeare's language. The language that is my focus here can be thought of as 'common' in various senses. It is the shared general resource of Shakespeare and his contemporaries, a resource that belongs to and is shaped by all of its speakers. It is also 'common' in the sense that it is ordinary and unpolished, the small words that pale next to arresting ear-catchers. In Shakespeare's works, these words shine in unexpected ways, especially when considered using features from linguistics-derived approaches. As I hope I have made clear, the methods applied in this book represent merely a sampling of those available to us. Strategies such as the consideration of types of utterances and conversational turn-taking represent only some of many possible methods of discourse analysis, for example. Moreover, I would like to emphasize that the respective approaches treated in each chapter are fundamentally interconnected. The boundary between sociolinguistics and pragmatics is porous, just as analyses of pragma-linguistic elements such as deictic markers cross into the territory of discourse analysis. My aim in this book is to emphasize different but related tools, so that we might continue to explore the uncommon effects of Shakespeare's common language.

NOTES

Introduction

1   See Howard and Strohm 549. The sense of the 'commons' as a nuisance to be managed is marvellously captured in a cutting phrase from *Henry VI, Part 3*: 'The common people swarm like summer flies' (2.6.8).

2   I have discussed these claims in greater detail in Kolentsis, 'Shakespeare's Linguistic Creativity'.

3   See Millward 230.

4   Mann further discusses the signification of 'common' as a shared plot of land and traces the ways that some rhetoricians shaped their arguments 'by figuring the English art of rhetoric as a common plot of land from which "euery sort" of person would be able to "reape," "gleane," and profit' (41).

5   Jonathan Hope and Michael Witmore point out the tendency to overlook function words in their discussion of the word 'the' in *Macbeth*: 'the determiner "the" … is exactly the sort of word literary critics tend not to comment on; indeed, it is exactly the sort of word even early quantitative and digital analysts excluded from their work on the assumption that it was too common to be interesting' (198). The matter of word of frequency and significance is discussed in greater detail in Chapter 4 of this book.

6   There has also been much productive recent work in other language-based approaches to early modern literature, especially those concerned with digital methodologies. See, for example, Craig and Greatly-Hirsch; Shore; and the continuing work of Jonathan Hope and Michael Witmore, collected at Wine Dark Sea.

7   Amelie Rorty suggests that our modern understanding of 'person' may be traced in part to 'theater, the dramatis personae

of the stage ... An actor dons masks, literally *per sonae*, that
through which the sound comes, the many roles he acts. A
person's roles and his place in the narrative devolve from the
choices that place him in a structural system, related to others.
The person thus comes to stand behind his roles, to select them
and to be judged by his choices and his capacities to act out his
personae in a total structure that is the unfolding of his drama'
(309, quoted in Herman, *Dramatic Discourse* 37–9).

Chapter 1

1 Some of the discussion featured in this chapter appeared in a different form in Kolentsis, '"Mark you / His absolute "shall"?'.

2 The noun 'voice' in *Coriolanus* owes something to the Latin *vox* as well as to 'contemporary Jacobean political procedures, specifically the customary method of parliamentary election'; Russ McDonald suggests that the Folio's consistent capitalization of 'Voice' and 'Voices' 'would seem to imply authorial intention' (*Shakespeare's Late Style* 53). Regardless of whether or not this emphasis is deliberate, 'voice' is a resonant term in the play, forging associations as various as cacophonous sound, political clout and the potential for individual or collective power.

3 Caius Martius's first lines show derision for the words of the people. To Menenius's explanation that they demand 'corn at their own rates, whereof they say / The city is well stored' (1.1.183–4), he ridicules both their words and the fact that Menenius grants credence to what 'they say': 'Hang 'em! "They say"?' (1.1.185). Such attention to the nuances of uttered statements will again be demonstrated in Act 3's 'absolute shall' scene and its aftermath, when the tribunes dub Coriolanus 'a traitor to the people': 'How? "Traitor"? ... Call me their "traitor", thou injurious tribune?' (3.3.66–9).

4 The Third Citizen frames this fear in terms of topographical distance, a metaphor that underscores the notion of individuals that are separate in every sense, from their goals for the future to their physical location: 'our wits are so diversely coloured. And

truly I think if all our wits were to issue out of one skull, they would fly east, west, north, south, and their consent of one direct way should be at once to all the points o'th'compass' (2.3.16–20).

5 Frans Plank remarks that 'the development of the English modals is a paradigm case of grammaticalization, showing in an exemplary manner how more or less ordinary lexical items are appropriated for the grammatical system' (308).

6 See Fitzmaurice, 'Tentativeness and Insistence' 11 and Hope, *Shakespeare's Grammar* 146.

7 It is not surprising that *shall* is the modal of choice for prophecy and God's commands in the first translations of the Vulgate Bible. As Brian Cummings observes, it is difficult to see this divine *shall* as a benign or impartial predictor: 'God's foreknowledge and God's predestination merge in the obligatory syntax of his modal auxiliaries' (*Literary Culture* 430). Rissanen notes that differences between *shall* and *will* were inscribed in the Wyliffite Bible translation, so that instances of 'will' were marked with volition (211).

8 For a discussion of *shall* and authority, see Bybee, Perkins and Pagliuca, esp. 262.

9 According to Austin's model, Sicinius's 'shall' violates the felicity conditions of a successful speech act. Austin's theory suggests that 'the particular persons and circumstances in a given case must be appropriate for the invocation of the particular procedure invoked' (15); otherwise, the speech act fails and is classified as a 'misapplication' (18). Coriolanus attempts to show that Sicinius, 'this Triton of the minnows' (3.1.90), does not constitute an 'appropriate' speaker.

10 See Skeat, who notes that the noun *peremptor* means 'a detroyer' (434). The roots of *peremptory* lie both in Latin *perimere* ('to take thoroughly') and *peremptorius* ('destructuve, decisive, final') (Partridge 191).

11 Additional evidence for the reversal is that it is now Coriolanus who resorts to this plaintiff position. Facing his prosecutors, he says 'First, hear me speak' (3.3.43) and his interrogative *shall* (which appeals to the authority of the addressee rather than the speaker) confirms the transfer of power: 'Shall I be charged no further than this present? / Must all determine here?' (3.3.46).

12 Compare North's account of this scene, in which the commanding 'shalts' are arranged differently: 'thou shalt see, my son, and trust to unto it, thou shalt no sooner march forward to assault thy country, but thy foot shall tread upon thy mother's womb, that brought thee first into this world' (141). It is only in Shakespeare's version that the commandment 'thou shalt not' is syntactically emphasized.

Chapter 2

1 The play's inconsistencies are also bound up with its troubled print history. First published in quarto in 1609, it was later reissued that same year with added introductory material. The publishers of the 1623 folio faced legal problems when setting *Troilus*, with the result that it was interrupted during typesetting and was eventually such a late inclusion that 'it has no page numbers and is not mentioned in the "catalogue of the severall Comedies, Histories, and Tragedies contained in this Volume" at the start of the folio' (Stern 120). The generic classification of the play is similarly unsettled: the 1609 Q as 'The history of Troylus and Cresseida,' while the 1623 F places it with the tragedies and gives it the title 'The tragedie of Troylus and Cressida.'

2 The abstract notion of 'face' is central to the model of politeness developed by Penelope Brown and Steven Levinson. 'Face' consists of two specific kinds of desires ('face-wants') attributed by interactants to one another; *negative face* is the desire to be unimpeded in one's actions, while *positive face* is the desire to be approved of.

3 Linda Charnes contends that the characters of *Troilus and Cressida* are stymied by the spectres of famous personas that they can never truly inhabit, arguing that subjectivity – 'the unstable heterogeneity that simultaneously constitutes and unfixes even the most "fixed" of names' – is in *Troilus* 'posited as the disruptive effect of simultaneous resistance, and subjection to, the determining force of famous names' (Charnes 74).

4   Cf. Grice. The maxim of quality: do not say what you believe to be false; do not say that for which you lack adequate evidence; and the maxim of quantity: make your contribution as informative as is required; do not make your contribution more informative than is required.

5   I am taking the principles of 'conversation' to be generalized to other aspects of speech: 'conversation should be considered the basic form of speech-exchange system ... In this light [more formal types such as] debate or ceremony would not be an independent polar type, but rather the most extreme transformation of conversation' (Sacks, Schegloff and Jefferson 47).

6   See Charnes, *Notorious Identity*.

7   See also the discussion of Coriolanus's interrogating questions in Chapter 1.

8   *Much Ado About Nothing* features one of Shakespeare's most memorable uses of this type of dialogue, where the ideally matched conversation partners Beatrice and Benedick spar and share nearly equally the role of pointed questioner and biting respondent.

9   It would appear that Cressida is a trailblazer in her tactics of conversational dissent. The *OED* cites this usage as the first recorded instance of 'excuse me' as a phrase of disagreement.

10 Another feature of note here is Cressida's couplet-sonnet soliloquy that ends the scene. We have just seen her held up as a Petrarchan object; when we witness her in the flesh, she culminates a brilliant display of speech by talking through this sonnet mode.

11 Discourse analysis is sometimes understood to encompass the macro-level of discourse, beyond lexical, grammatical and syntactical elements: 'the study of language above the level of a sentence, of the ways sentences combine to create meaning, coherence, and accomplish purposes. However, even a single sentence or utterance can be analyzed as a "communication" or as an "action", and not just as a sentence structure whose "literal meaning" flows from the nature of grammar' (Gee and Handford 1). Halliday focuses on smaller-scale elements.

12 The implication of will as a dangerous intermediate stage between control and indulgence is evident in Nestor's warning that 'Ajax is grown self-willed' (1.3.189). Indeed, in Thersites' estimation, Ajax makes the full transition to barbaric creature: 'He's grown a very land-fish, language-less, a monster' (3.3.260–1).

13 Cressida's self-blazon here strongly recalls Troilus's praise of 'her eyes, her hair, her cheek, her gait, her voice' (1.1.51), another moment of echo or cohesion that subtly overwrites her characterization by others with her own response.

14 Cressida's uses the *I will* construction only eight times in the play; contrast this to Troilus, who uses it almost twice as often, and Thersites, who uses *I will* more than twenty times.

15 Adelman claims that Cressida's character gradually becomes a cipher in the play, moving from openness to opacity. Such voyeuristic distance aligns the audience and Troilus, so that Cressida becomes equally unreachable to both: 'we take our places as the furthest removed of the spectators as we watch Thersites watching Ulysses watching Troilus watching Cressida. That is, Cressida seems to betray *us* at the same time she betrays Troilus; our relationship with her is broken off as sharply as hers with Troilus' ('This Is and Is Not Cressid' 128).

16 Cressida here recalls one of Shakespeare's most resolutely defiant female characters, Cleopatra, who refuses instructions not to follow Anthony onto the battlefield: 'Speak not against it, / I will not stay behind' (3.7.18–19).

17 The first waking moments following the consummation of the relationship are characterized by hints that Troilus wants to distance himself from Cressida. He tries repeatedly to send her back to bed, a suggestion that Cressida presciently reads as rejection: 'Are you a-weary of me?' (4.2.9).

18 Magnusson identifies an important qualification by noting that relationships are reinforced as well as created in linguistic encounters. Citing Bourdieu's argument 'that "interpersonal" relations are never, except in appearance, individual-to-individual relationships and that the truth of the interaction is never entirely contained in the interaction', Magnusson asserts that it is 'misleading to suggest that the individual speakers …

are continuously producing, through their own independent initiatives, the coordinated practices of self-maintenance', and directs attention towards 'the inscription in the conversational organization of the characters' relative social positions' (*Shakespeare and Social Dialogue* 147).

Chapter 3

1. As Charles R. Forker observes in the notes to the Arden edition of *Richard II* (2002), the truncated metre of Northumberland's line also invites attention because it requires a beat mid-line: 'The pause, which is dramatically effective, is probably intentional' (3.3.10 n.10).
2. See Stein. For a discussion of Donne, see the introduction to Dubrow's *Deixis in the Early Modern English Lyric*.
3. Also relevant here is Charles Sanders Peirce's concept of the index, 'a sign which refers to the object that it denotes by virtue of being really affected by that object', or 'which relates to the pointed-to object through physical contiguity' (such as a knock at the door indicating someone outside it) (Elam 21–2).
4. Gurr, 'You and Thou'; Hope, 'Second person singular pronouns'; Freedman, *Power and Passion*.
5. Herman's most salient work on deixis is *Dramatic Discourse: Dialogue as Interaction in Plays* and 'Deixis and Space in Drama.'
6. 'Origo' is a term used in pragmatics to describe the centre, or reference point, on which deictic relationships are based.
7. Elam claims that a drama is characterized by progression, and such movement is tracked by the deictic markers that 'actualize' the dramatic world: 'It is evident that the possible worlds of the drama are never simple and static states of affairs but, rather, complex successions of states' (117). Similarly, Herman points to the centrality of space and time to dramatic worlds, and notes that the element of flux is particularly significant: 'spatio-temporal and participant coordinates of the fictional world are open to shifts and change, whereas the wider performance centre remains "constant," within performance time and place,

to a greater degree'. It is through deixis that such change is represented, and that the contrast between onstage fictional space and time and performance space and time is established: 'each performance presupposes a different "now", a different deictic centre' ('Deixis and Space' 30).

8   Cf. the deposition scene, when York isolates Bolingbroke's name as he demands Richard's resignation: 'To do that office of thine own good will / Which tired majesty did make thee offer – / The resignation of thy state and crown / To Henry Bolingbroke' (4.1.178–81).

9   England and Englishness are subject to many claims of propriety in *Richard II*, from Richard's 'my land' and 'our England', to Bolingbroke's 'my English breath' (3.1.20), Mowbray's 'my native English' (1.3.160), the gardener's 'our sea-walled garden' (3.4.43), and Gaunt's 'this other Eden … this dear dear land' (2.1.42, 57).

10 This faith prompts the misguided words of reassurance offered by the Bishop of Carlisle: 'Fear not, my lord. That Power that made you king / Hath power to keep you king in spite of all' (3.2.27–8). Even divine power, which presumably sits atop the scale of relative power, proves hollow in this case.

11 Anthropologist Victor Turner identifies rituals as 'cultural performances', acts as diverse as 'prayers, ritual readings and recitations, rites and ceremonies, [and] festivals' (23). He argues that ritual is enacted at the border of the social world; it 'is not unidirectional and "positive" in the sense that the performative genre merely "reflects" or "expresses" the social system or the cultural configuration, or at any rate their key relationships – but that it is reciprocal and reflective – in the sense that the performance is often a critique, direct or veiled, of the social life it grows out of, and evaluation (with lively possibilities of rejection) of the way society handles history' (22).

12 See Bourdieu's discussion of ritual and its capacity to generate comfort in the face of 'metaphysical anxiety' (*Theory of Practice* 115).

13 Marjorie Garber suggests that 'with this broken ceremony Richard symbolizes, to the audience in the theatre as well as that on the stage, the vulnerability of his idea of kingship. In *Hamlet*

broken ceremonies of this kind will be termed "maimed rites," and this is indeed a maimed rite, the failure of an idea' (243).

14 We observe Richard incorporating the 'language of the body' elsewhere in the play. One notable instance occurs when he calls out Bolingbroke on his sedition: 'Up, cousin, up. Your heart is up, I know, / Thus high at least, although your knee be low' (3.3.193–4). The word 'thus' prescribes the gesture of touching the sought-after crown, a visual effect that harshly exposes Bolingbroke's ambition and prepares us for the discomfiting spectacle of the deposition scene, when the crown will be suspended between Richard and Bolingbroke.

15 Hanks observes that performance-based rituals across cultures are 'accompanied by some paraphernalia' (*Intertexts* 232). Here, the king's warder serves as the central ritual object, a visual sign of the king's commanding and peremptory voice.

16 The speech exemplifies Stanley Cavell's notion of 'passionate utterance', explained by Sarah Beckwith as a type of performative utterance absent the typical form and felicity conditions: 'If, in performative utterance the procedure must be executed correctly and concretely, such requirements are utterly moot in the case of passionate utterance for there is no agreed procedure' (115).

17 Ernst Cassirer's observation that 'deictic particles' such as *here, there* and *this* 'are intimately fused with the direct gesture of showing, whereby a particular object is singled out from the sphere of immediate perception' (338) is also relevant here. The crown is singled out, 'set apart' like the very act of ritual in which it is embedded, acquiring the significance peculiar to an object being observed from a fresh perspective.

18 As Berger notes, 'awareness of this betrayal is inscribed in Richard's language … it is the source of his self-contempt and his often sarcastic use of Christian rhetoric' (51).

19 These actions correspond to examples cited by Hanks as typical of worship rituals, such as 'begging, requesting, recounting, cleansing' ('I request'; 'I address you all'). Hanks also notes the prevalence of self-situating within the physical site of the ritual: 'I am seated at the foot of your altar' (*Language and Communicative Practices* 232).

20 Many critics have pointed to the Marlovian echoes in the mirror scene, which recalls the moment when Faustus sees the conjured Helen of Troy: 'Was this the face that launched a thousand ships / And burnt the topless towers of Ilium?' (Marlowe, *Doctor Faustus* 5.1.90–1). While there are rich possibilities for dramatic irony in the overlap between the respective scenes, there are also pertinent differences. Whereas Faustus's *this* marks the potency of the vision (Helen is indeed physically proximal, close enough to 'kiss'), Richard's marks the starting point from which his own identity recedes, moving from proximity to distance.

Chapter 4

1 As translated by William J. Ziobro.

2 An earlier discussion of the broad category of early modern English grammar appeared in '"Grammar Rules" in the Sonnets: Sidney and Shakespeare', but my discussion here is extended and altered.

3 On the scope of grammar, see Hope, *Shakespeare and Language* 34–7.

4 As Colin Burrow notes, 'St. Paul's school, along with Westminster and Eton, certainly provided the model for the statutes of many Tudor grammar schools, but this does not mean that all schools were like them in practice. Even William Lily, the first High Master of St. Paul's and the author of a Latin grammar which was to be prescribed by statute as the only one to be used in schools, notes that "The varietie of teaching is diuers yet, and always wil be"' (12).

5 Whittington's 'Shakespeare's Grammar: Latin, Literacy, and the Vernacular' features a thorough account of the history and influence of *Lily's Grammar* in Shakespeare's England. The essay also provides valuable insight into the disorder and confusion inherent in the so-called Royal Grammar. Not only did it go through scores of different editions, but the authoritative 1548 edition 'included not one but two separate introductions to grammar, one in English and one in Latin,

pieced together by the king's committee of learned men from material written by at least five authors, whose incongruous compositions were never intended to lie between the covers of one book' (89).

6   While early modern humanists emphasized the value of widely available educational opportunities, many children were excluded from the experience of grammar schools. Places in grammar schools were, of course, available only to boys, and most of the influx of new pupils in sixteenth-century England derived from middle-class families.

7   The matter of early modern education has long been the object of keen scholarly attention, beginning with T.W. Baldwin's foundational two-volume *William Shakespeare's Small Latine and Less Greeke* (1944) and bolstered by Joel Altman's *The Tudor Play of Mind* (1978) and Anthony Grafton and Lisa Jardine's *From Humanism to Humanities: Education and the Liberal Arts in Fifteenth- and Sixteenth-Century Europe* (1986). More recently, the work of scholars such as Rebecca Bushnell, Jeff Dolven and Lynn Enterline has helped to reshape our understanding of the early modern English classroom, particularly in regard to the relationships to performativity and authority instilled in young pupils.

8   See Enterline, who argues that the monitoring of academic performance (of oneself and one's classmates) is a key skill developed within the context of the humanist grammar school (40–7).

9   See also Barkan's discussion of this scene: 'The learned fool treats his hapless interlocutor to an almost complete performance of the grammar-school education than an Arden rustic cannot have experienced for real' (38).

10 The Ganymede story 'figures in one of a large number of contingent narratives about love and lust interpolated by Ovid into the story of Orpheus in Books 10 and 11 of the *Metamorphoses*' (Orgel 143). As Orgel notes, Shakespeare alters all of the names from his source in Lodge's *Rosalynde* except those of his 'heroine and her alter ego. Ganymede was as indispensable as Rosalind' (143).

11 Leonard Barkan notes that 'Terence formed one of the bases for Latin instruction all over Europe because his dialogue was thought to give the fullest impression of the way Latin was actually spoken' (34).

12 The increased use of subordinating conjunctions like *if* was a distinctive marker of early modern English: 'A syntactical development in early New English (1450–1750) was its improved co-ordination and subordination of clauses. Transitions within paragraphs were eased by the use of relative pronouns derived from the interrogatives *who* and *which*, as well as by a variety of new prepositions and conjunctions. Prepositional phrases took the place of the inflected cases and adverbs. Add to these changes the increased use of auxiliaries … and the employment of the primaries be, do, and have in the formulation of moods and tenses' (Partridge 19).

13 Barber notes that *an/and* for *if*, while standard in Shakespeare's time, faded over the course of the seventeenth century and was dated by the eighteenth century: 'By Congreve's time … this usage had become old-fashioned. In *The Way of the World*, all the examples of *an* "if" occur in the speech of Sir Wilfull Witwould, the unpolished country squire. The smart ladies and gentlemen of London, and their servants, invariably use *if*, and even Sir Wilfull himself uses *if* more often than *an*' (208).

14 The *if*-clause has been the subject of some critical attention in Shakespeare studies. Madeleine Doran explores the dramatic effect of Iago's *if*s in *Shakespeare's Dramatic Language* (1976), and Maura Slattery Kuhn, in a 1977 article for *Shakespeare Quarterly*, discusses the *if*s of *As You Like It*. More recently, Jonathan P. Lamb considers the *if*-clause in Shakespeare in *Shakespeare in the Marketplace of Words* (2017). My thinking and discussion in this chapter is indebted to these diverse and discerning analyses. I am also grateful for the insights of Nick Moschovakis, who discusses *if* and other conditional forms in a paper for the 'Shakespeare's Language: Changing Methods' seminar at the 2019 meeting of the Shakespeare Association of America.

15 See Scott Kaiser, who uses these examples and beautifully summarizes Shakespeare's *if*s: '"If" can be a beginning, a fork

in the road, or an end. "If" can defend the past, change the present, or predict the future' (223).

16 According to the digital tool WordHoard, the plays with the highest concentration of *if*s are as follows: *Othello*, 139; *As You Like It*, 138; *Much Ado About Nothing*, 124; *The Merchant of Venice*, 120; *Measure for Measure*, 112; *Twelfth Night*, 104. Othello's position at the top of the list is notable, given Iago's dependence on dissembling *if*s (for further discussion, see Madeleine Doran, 'Iago's *If* – Conditional and Subjunctive in Othello' in *Shakespeare's Dramatic Language*).

17 *Open Source Shakespeare* lists *if*s by character as follows: Rosalind, 27; Touchstone, 12; Celia, 8; Orlando, 7. Compare to Lear's 15; Hamlet's 34; and Iago's 38.

REFERENCES

Adamson, Sylvia. 'From Emphatic Deixis to Emphatic Narrative: Stylistaion and (De)subjectivisation as Processes of Language Change'. *Subjectivity and Subjectivisation: An Introduction.* Cambridge: Cambridge University Press, 1995, 195–224.

Adamson, Sylvia. 'Literary Language'. *The Cambridge History of the English Language*, vol. 3. Ed. Roger Lass. Cambridge: Cambridge University Press, 1999, 539–653.

Adamson, Sylvia. 'Understanding Shakespeare's Grammar: Studies in Small Words'. *Reading Shakespeare's Dramatic Language.* Eds Sylvia Adamson, Lynette Hunter, Lynne Magnusson, Ann Thompson, and Katie Wales. London: Arden, 2001, 210–36.

Adelman, Janet. '"This Is and Is Not Cressid": The Characterization of Cressida'. *The (M)other Tongue.* Eds Shirley Nelson Garner, Claire Kahane, and Madelon Sprengnether. Ithaca, NY: Cornell University Press, 1985.

Altman, Joel B. *The Tudor Play of Mind: Rhetorical Inquiry and the Development of Elizabethan Drama.* Berkeley, CA: University of California Press, 1978.

Arnovick, Leslie K. *The Development of Future Constructions in English.* New York, NY: Peter Lang, 1990.

Austin, J.L. *How To Do Things With Words.* Cambridge, MA: Harvard University Press, 1962.

Bakhtin, M.M. *Rabelais and His World.* Trans. Helene Iswolsky. Cambridge, MA: MIT University Press, 1968.

Bakhtin, M.M. *The Dialogic Imagination.* Ed. Michael Holquist. Trans. Caryl Emerson and Michael Holquist. Austin, TX: University of Texas Press, 1981.

Baldwin, T.W. *William Shakespeare's Small Latine and Less Greeke.* 2 vols. Urbana, OH: University of Illinois Press, 1944.

Barber, Charles. *Early Modern English.* Edinburgh: Edinburgh University Press, 1997.

Barkan, Leonard. 'What did Shakespeare Read?' *The Cambridge Companion to Shakespeare.* Eds Margreta de Grazia and Stanley Wells. Cambridge: Cambridge University Press, 2001, 31–47.

Beckwith, Sarah. *Shakespeare and the Grammar of Forgiveness*. Ithaca, NY: Cornell University Press, 2011.
Benveniste, Emile. *Problems in General Linguistics*. Trans. Mary Elizabeth Meek. Coral Gables, FL: University of Miami Press, 1971.
Berger, Harry Jr. *Imaginary Audition: Shakespeare on Stage and Page*. Berkeley, CA: University of California Press, 1989.
Black, Joseph, et al. eds. *The Broadview Anthology of British Literature*, vol. 1. 2nd edn. Peterborough, ONT: Broadview, 2009.
Bourdieu, Pierre. *Outline of a Theory of Practice*. Trans. Richard Nice. Cambridge: Cambridge University Press, 1977.
Brisard, Frank. 'Meaning and Use in Grammar'. *Grammar, Meaning and Pragmatics*. Eds Frank Brisard, Jan-Ola Ostman, and Jef Verschueren. Amsterdam: John Benjamins, 2009, 1–15.
Brown, Penelope and Stephen C. Levinson. *Politeness: Some Universals in Language Usage*. Cambridge: Cambridge University Press, 1987.
Bullokar, William. *Bref Grammar of English*. London: Edmund Bollifant, 1586.
Burrow, Colin. 'Introduction'. *The Oxford Shakespeare: The Complete Sonnets and Poems*. Oxford: Oxford University Press, 2002, 1–158.
Bushnell, Rebecca W. *A Culture of Teaching: Early Modern Humanism in Theory and Practice*. Ithaca, NY: Cornell University Press, 1996.
Bybee, Joan L., Revere Perkins, and William Pagliuca. *The Evolution of Grammar*. Chicago, MI: University of Chicago Press, 1994.
Caesar, Philip. *A General Discourse Against the Damnable Sect of Vsurers* (1578). *Early English Books Online*.
Calvo, Clara. 'In Defence of Celia: Discourse Analysis and Women's Discourse in *As You Like It*'. *Essays and Studies* 47 (1994): 91–115.
Cassirer, Ernst. *The Philosophy of Symbolic Forms*, vol. 1. Trans. Ralph Manheim. New Haven, CT: Yale University Press, 1953.
Chapman, Siobahn. *Pragmatics*. Basingstoke: Palgrave, 2011.
Charnes, Linda. *Notorious Identity: Materializing the Subject in Shakespeare*. Cambridge, MA: Harvard University Press, 1993.
Coulthard, Malcolm. *An Introduction to Discourse Analysis*. London: Longman, 1977.

Coverdale, Miles. *Certain most Godly, Fruitful, and Comfortable Letters of Such True Saintes and Holy Martyrs of God* (1564). *Early English Books Online.*

Cox, Leonard. *The Arte or Crafte of Rhetoryk*. London: Robert Redmond, 1532.

Craig, Hugh. 'Grammatical Modality in English Plays from the 1580s to the 1640s'. *English Literary Renaissance* 30 (2000): 32–54.

Craig, Hugh and Brett Greatly-Hirsch. *Style, Computers, and Early Modern Drama: Beyond Authorship*. Cambridge: Cambridge University Press, 2017.

Culpeper, Jonathan and Dawn Archer. 'Requests and Directness in Early Modern English Trial Proceedings and Play-Texts, 1640–1760'. *Speech Acts in the History of English*. Eds Andreas H. Jucker and Irma Taavitsainen. Amsterdam: John Benjamins, 2008, 45–84.

Cummings, Brian. *The Literary Culture of the Reformation: Grammar and Grace*. Oxford: Oxford University Press, 2002.

Cummings, Brian. *Mortal Thoughts: Religion, Secularity, and Identity in Early Modern Culture*. Oxford: Oxford University Press, 2013.

Derrida, Jacques. *Of Grammatology*. Trans. Gayatri Chakravorty Spivak. Baltimore, MD: Johns Hopkins University Press, 1974.

Dolven, Jeff. *Scenes of Instruction in Renaissance Romance*. Chicago, MI: University of Chicago Press, 2007.

Doran, Madeleine. *Shakespeare's Dramatic Language*. Madison, WI: University of Wisconsin Press, 1976.

Eggins, Suzanne. *An Introduction to Systemic Functional Linguistics*. 2nd edn. London: Continuum, 2004.

Eggins, Suzanne and Diana Slade. *Analyzing Casual Conversation*. London: Cassell, 1997.

Elam, Keir. *The Semiotics of Theatre and Drama*. London: Methuen, 1980.

Enterline, Lynn. *Shakespeare's Schoolroom: Rhetoric, Discipline, Emotion*. Philadelphia, PA: Penn University Press, 2012.

Fabb, Nigel. *Linguistics and Literature*. Oxford: Blackwell, 1997.

Facchinetti, Roberta. 'The Modal Verb *shall* between Grammar and Usage in the Nineteenth Century'. *The History of English in a Social Context*. Eds Dieter Kastovsky and Arthur Mettinger. Berlin: Mouton de Gruyter, 2000, 115–33.

Fitzmaurice, Susan M. 'Tentativeness and insistence in the expression of politeness in Margaret Cavendish's *Sociable Letters*'. *Language and Literature* 9 (2000): 7–24.

Fitzmaurice, Susan M. *The Familiar Letter in Early Modern English: A Pragmatic Approach*. Amsterdam: John Benjamins, 2002.

Freedman, Penelope. *Power and Passion in Shakespeare's Pronouns*. London: Ashgate, 2007.

Furrow, Melissa. 'Listening Reader and Impotent Speaker: The Role of Deixis in Literature'. *Language and Style* 21 (1988): 365–78.

Garber, Marjorie. *Shakespeare After All*. New York, NY: Pantheon, 2004.

Gee, James Paul and Michael Handford, eds. *The Routledge Handbook of Discourse Analysis*. New York, NY: Routledge, 2012.

Geurts, Bart. *Quality Implicatures*. Cambridge: Cambridge University Press, 2010.

Görlach, Manfred. 'Regional and Social Variation'. *The Cambridge History of the English Language*, vol. 3. Ed. Roger Lass. Cambridge: Cambridge University Press, 1999.

Grafton, Anthony and Lisa Jardine. *From Humanism to the Humanities: Education and the Liberal Arts in Fifteenth- and Sixteenth-Century Europe*. Cambridge, MA: Harvard University Press, 1986.

Grice, H. Paul. 'Logic and Conversation'. *Speech Acts*. Eds Peter Cole and Jerry L. Morgan. New York, NY: Academic Press, 1975, 41–58.

Gurr, Andrew. 'Textual Analysis'. *King Richard II*. By William Shakespeare. Ed. Andrew Gurr. Cambridge: Cambridge University Press, 2003.

Gurr, Andrew. 'You and Thou in Shakespeare's Sonnets'. *Essays in Criticism* 32 (1982): 9–25.

Gwosdek, Hedwig, ed. *Lily's Grammar of Latin in English: An introduction of the eyght partes of speche and the construction of the same, William Lily*. Oxford: Oxford University Press, 2013.

Halliday, M.A.K. *Linguistic Studies of Text and Discourse*. Ed. Jonathan Webster. London: Continuum, 2002.

Hanafi, Rhoda. 'Theory of the Subject as Pronoun'. *Tessera* 5 (1988): 91–105.

Hanks, William F. *Intertexts: Writing on Language, Utterance, and Context*. Lantham, NY: Rowman & Littlefield, 2000.

Hanks, William F. *Language and Communicative Practices*. Boulder, CO: Westview, 1996.

Hanks, William F. 'Notes on Semantics in Linguistic Practice'. *Bourdieu: Critical Perspectives*. Ed. Craig Calhoun, Edward LiPuma, and Mosihe Postone. Chicago, IL: University of Chicago Press, 1993, 139–55.

Hanks, William F. *Referential Practice: Language and Lived Space Among the Maya*. Chicago, MI: University of Chicago Press, 1990.

Herman, Vimala. 'Deixis and Space in Drama'. *Social Semiotics* 7.3 (1997): 269–83.

Herman, Vimala. *Dramatic Discourse: Dialogue as Interaction in Plays*. London: Routledge, 1995.

Hodge, Robert and Gunther Kress. *Social Semiotics*. Ithaca, NY: Cornell University Press, 1988.

Hope, Jonathan. 'Second Person Singular Pronouns in Records of Early Modern "Spoken" English'. *Neuphilologische Mitteilungen* (1993): 83–100.

Hope, Jonathan. *Shakespeare and Language: Reason, Eloquence and Artifice in the Renaissance*. London: Methuen, 2010.

Hope, Jonathan. *Shakespeare's Grammar*. London: Arden, 2003.

Hope, Jonathan. 'Shakespeare's "Natiue English"'. *A Companion to Shakespeare*. Ed. David Scott Kastan. Oxford: Blackwell, 1999, 239–55.

Hope, Jonathan and Michael Witmore. 'The Language of *Macbeth*'. *Macbeth: The State of Play*. Ed. Ann Thompson. London: Bloomsbury, 2014, 183–208.

Howard, Jean E. and Paul Strohm. 'Imaginary Commons'. *Journal of Medieval and Early Modern Studies* 37.3 (2007): 549–77.

Hymes, D.H. 'On Communicative Competence'. *Sociolinguistics: Selected Readings*. Eds J.B. Pride and J. Holmes. Harmondsworth: Penguin, 1972, 269–93.

Iser, Wolfgang. *Staging Politics: The Lasting Impact of Shakespeare's Histories*. New York, NY: Columbia University Press, 1993.

James, Francis. *Semantics of the English Subjunctive*. Vancouver: University of British Columbia Press, 1986.

James, Heather. 'Shakespeare's Learned Heroines in Ovid's Schoolroom'. *Shakespeare and the Classics*. Eds Charles Martindale and A.B. Taylor. Cambridge: Cambridge University Press, 2004, 66–85.

Kaiser, Scott. *Shakespeare's Wordcraft*. New York, NY: Limelight, 2007.

Kolentsis, Alysia. '"Grammar Rules" in the Sonnets: Sidney and Shakespeare'. *The Oxford Handbook of Shakespeare's Poetry*.

Ed. Jonathan Post, Oxford: Oxford University Press, 2013. 168–184.

Kolentsis, Alysia. '"Mark you/His absolute shall?": Multitudinous Tongues and Contested Words in *Coriolanus*'. *Shakespeare Survey* 62 (2009): 141–50.

Kolentsis, Alysia. 'Shakespeare's Linguistic Creativity: A Reappraisal'. *Literature Compass* 11.4 (2014): 258–66.

Kuhn, Maura Slattery. 'Much Virtue in "If."' *Shakespeare Quarterly* 28 (1977): 40–50.

Lamb, Jonathan P. *Shakespeare in the Marketplace of Words*. Cambridge: Cambridge University Press, 2017.

Lamb, Mary Ellen. 'Apologizing for Pleasure in Sidney's "Apology for Poetry": The Nurse of Abuse Meets the Tudor Grammar School'. *Criticism* 36.4 (1994): 499–519.

Leggatt, Alexander. *Shakespeare's Political Drama*. London: Routledge, 1988.

Levinson, Stephen C. *Pragmatics*. Cambridge: Cambridge University Press, 1983.

Liberman, Anatoly. 'A Few More of Our Shortest Words: "If," "Of," and "Both"'. *The Oxford Etymologist*. Oxford University Press. https://blog.oup.com/2017/08/if-etymology/ (accessed 14 September 2018).

Linell, Per and Thomas Luckmann. 'Asymmetries in Dialogue: Some Conceptual Preliminaries'. *Asymmetries in Dialogue*. Eds Ivana Markova and Klaus Foppa. Hemel Hempstead: Harvester Wheatsheaf, 1991, 1–20.

McDonald, Russ. *Shakespeare's Late Style*. Cambridge: Cambridge University Press, 2006.

Machan, Tim William and Charles T. Scott, eds. *English in its Social Contexts: Essays in Historical Sociolinguistics*. New York, NY: Oxford University Press, 1992.

Magnusson, Lynne. 'A Pragmatics for Interpreting Shakespeare's Sonnets 1 to 20: Dialogue Scripts and Erasmian Intertexts'. *Methods in Historical Pragmatics*. Eds Susan M. Fitzmaurice and Irma Taavitsainen. Berlin: Mouton de Gruyter, 2007, 167–84.

Magnusson, Lynne. *Shakespeare and Social Dialogue: Dramatic Language and Elizabethan Letters*. Cambridge: Cambridge University Press, 1999.

Maguire, Laurie E. 'Performing Anger: The Anatomy of Abuse(s) in *Troilus and Cressida*'. *Renaissance Drama* 31 (2002): 153–83.

Mann, Jenny C. *Outlaw Rhetoric: Figuring Vernacular Eloquence in Shakespeare's England*. Ithaca, NY: Cornell University Press, 2012.

Marlowe, Christopher. *Doctor Faustus (A-Text)*. In *Doctor Faustus and Other Plays*. Eds David Bevington and Eric Rasmussen. Oxford: Oxford University Press, 1995. 137–83.

Millward, Linda C. *A Biography of the English Language*. 2nd edn. Orlando, FL: Harcourt Brace, 1996.

Mitchell, Linda C. *Grammar Wars: Language as Cultural Battlefield in 17th and 18th Century England*. Aldershot: Ashgate, 2001.

Mulcaster, Richard. *The First Part of the Elementary*. 1582. Menston: Scolar Press, 1970.

Nash, Walter. 'Changing the Guard at Elsinore'. *Language, Discourse, and Literature: An Introductory Reader in Discourse Analysis*. Eds Ronald Carter and Paul Simpson. New York, NY: Routledge, 1989, 21–40.

Nevalainen, Terttu. *An Introduction to Early Modern English*. Oxford: Oxford University Press, 2006.

North, Thomas. *Plutarch's Lives of the Noble Grecians and Romans*. Ed. Paul Turner. Carbondale, IL: Southern Illinois University Press, 1963.

Ong, Walter J. 'Latin Language Study as a Renaissance Puberty Rite'. *Studies in Philology* 56.2 (1959): 103–24.

Orgel, Stephen. 'The Further Adventures of Ganymede'. *Childhood, Education and the Stage in Early Modern England*. Eds Richard Preiss and Deanne Williams. Cambridge: Cambridge University Press, 2017, 143–61.

Parker, Patricia. *Shakespeare from the Margins: Language, Culture, Context*. Chicago, IL: University of Chicago Press, 1996.

Partridge, Eric. *Origins: A Short Etymological Dictionary of Modern English*. 4th edn. London: Routledge and Kegan Paul, 1966.

Perkins, Michael R. *Modal Expressions in English*. London: Frances Pinter, 1983.

Plank, Frans. 'The Modals Story Retold'. *Studies in Language* 8.3 (1984): 305–64.

Potter, Ursula. 'To School or Not to School: Tudor Views on Education in Drama and Literature'. *Parergon* 25.1 (2008): 103–21.

Quirk, Randolph, et al. *A Grammar of Contemporary English*. London: Longman, 1972.

Rissanen, Matti. 'Syntax'. *The Cambridge History of the English Language*, vol. 3, *1476–1776*. Ed. Roger Lass. Cambridge: Cambridge University Press, 1999.

Rorty, Amelie Oksenberg. 'A Literary Postscript: Characters, Persons, Selves, Individuals'. *The Identities of Persons*. Ed. Amelie Oksenberg Rorty. Berkeley, CA: University of California Press, 1976, 301–24.

Ruthrof, Horst. *The Body in Language*. London: Cassell, 2000.

Sacks, Harvey, Emanuel A. Schegloff, and Gail Jefferson. 'A Simplest Systematics for the Organization of Turn Taking for Conversation'. *Studies in the Organization of Conversational Interaction*. Ed. Jim Schenkein. New York, NY: Academic Press, 1978, 7–55.

Sander, Nicholas. *The rocke of the Churche wherein the primacy of S. Peter and of his successours the Bishops of Rome is proued out of Gods worde*. 1567. *Early English Books Online*.

Saussure, Ferdinand de. *Course in General Linguistics*. Trans. Wade Baskin. 1913. London: Fontana-Collins, 1974.

Shakespeare, William. *Antony and Cleopatra*. *The Norton Shakespeare*, vol. 2. Ed. Stephen Greenblatt et al. New York, NY: Norton, 1997, 899–987.

Shakespeare, William. *As You Like It*. Ed. Juliet Dusinberre. London: Arden, 2006.

Shakespeare, William. *As You Like It*. Ed. Leah S. Marcus. New York, NY: Norton, 2012.

Shakespeare, William. *Complete Sonnets and Poems*. Ed. Colin Burrow. Oxford: Oxford University Press, 2002.

Shakespeare, William. *Coriolanus*. Ed. Lee Bliss. Cambridge: Cambridge University Press, 2000.

Shakespeare, William. *Coriolanus*. Ed. Peter Holland. London: Arden, 2018.

Shakespeare, William. *Hamlet*. *The Norton Shakespeare*, vol. 2. Eds Stephen Greenblatt et al. New York, NY: Norton, 1997, 103–204.

Shakespeare, William. *Hamlet*. Ed. Susanne L. Wofford. Boston, MA: Bedford, 1994.

Shakespeare, William. *1 Henry IV*. *The Norton Shakespeare*, vol. 1. Eds Stephen Greenblatt et al. New York, NY: Norton, 1997, 1177–320.

Shakespeare, William. *2 Henry IV*. *The Norton Shakespeare*, vol. 1. Ed.s Stephen Greenblatt et al. New York, NY: Norton, 1997, 1321–470.

Shakespeare, William. *Julius Caesar*. Ed. David Daniell. London: Arden, 1998.
Shakespeare, William. *King Lear*. Ed. R.A. Foakes. London: Arden, 1997.
Shakespeare, William. *King Richard II*. Ed. Andrew Gurr. Cambridge: Cambridge University Press, 2003.
Shakespeare, William. *King Richard II*. Ed. Charles Forker. London: Arden, 2002.
Shakespeare, William. *Measure for Measure*. *The Norton Shakespeare*, vol. 2. Eds Stephen Greenblatt et al. New York, NY: Norton, 1997, 305–74.
Shakespeare, William. *Richard II*. Eds Barbara A. Mowat and Paul Werstine. New York: Washington Square Press, 1996.
Shakespeare, William. *Shakespeare's Sonnets*. Ed. Katherine Duncan Jones. London: Arden, 1997.
Shakespeare, William. *Shakespeare's Sonnets and Poetry*. Eds Barbara A. Mowat and Paul Werstine. New York, NY: Washington Square Press, 2006.
Shakespeare, William. *The Oxford Shakespeare: The Complete Works*. 2nd edn. Eds Stanley Wells, Gary Taylor, John Jowett, and William Montgomery. Oxford: Oxford University Press, 2005.
Shakespeare, William. *Troilus and Cressida*. Ed. David Bevington. London: Arden, 2001.
Shakespeare, William. *Troilus and Cressida*. Ed. Anthony B. Dawson. Cambridge: Cambridge University Press, 2003.
Shakespeare, William. *Troilus and Cressida*. Ed. Kenneth Palmer. London: Methuen, 1982.
Shaughnessy, Robert. 'As If'. *Shakespeare Bulletin* 35.1 (2018): 37–48.
Shore, Daniel. *Cyberformalism: Histories of Linguistic Forms in the Digital Archives*. Baltimore, MD: Johns Hopkins University Press, 2018.
Siemon, James R. *Word Against Word: Shakespearean Utterance*. Amherst, MA: University of Massachusetts Press, 2002.
Skeat, Walter W. *An Etymological Dictionary of the English Language*. Oxford: Clarendon, 1882.
Stein, Gertrude. *Everybody's Autobiography*. 1937. New York, NY: Random House, 1973.
Stern, Tiffany. *Making Shakespeare*. London: Routledge, 2004.

Tannen, Deborah. 'Silence as Conflict Management in Fiction and Drama: Pinter's *Betrayal* and a Short Story, "Great Wits"'. *Conflict Talk*. Ed. Allen D. Grimshaw. Cambridge: Cambridge University Press, 1990, 260–79.

Tedeschi, Philip J. 'If: A Study of English Conditional Sentences'. PhD diss., University of Michigan, 1976. Ann Arbor, MI: Xerox University Microfilms, 1976.

Traugott, E.C. and Richard B. Dasher. *Regularity in Semantic Change*. Cambridge: Cambridge University Press, 2002.

Turner, Victor. *The Anthropology of Performance*. New York, NY: PAJ Publications, 1987.

Verdonk, Peter. *Stylistics*. Oxford: Oxford University Press, 2002.

Visser, F. Th. *An Historical Syntax of the English Language*, vol 3. Leiden: Brill, 1969.

Werth, Paul. 'Introduction'. *Conversation and Discourse*. Ed. Paul Werth. London: Croon Helm, 1981, 9–15.

Whittington, Leah. 'Shakespeare's Grammar: Latin, Literacy, and the Vernacular'. *The Routledge Research Companion to Shakespeare and Classical Literature*. Eds Sean Keilen and Nick Moschovakis. Abingdon: Routledge, 2017, 78–106.

Wine Dark Sea. winedarksea.org (accessed 10 July 2019).

INDEX

Individual words discussed in the text are italicised (e.g. *shall*, *will*). Page references for notes are in the format 162 n.4.

ability 45
action 27–28, 37–40, 42, 116
　future 122–3
　versus talk 25, 28, 84
Adamson, Sylvia 6, 9, 14, 22, 33, 123
adjectives, possessive 129
adverbs 126, 152
agency 40, 45, 84, 123–4, 128
aggression 28–9, 45–54, 113, 155
　threat 34, 113–14
Alexander (*Troilus and Cressida*) 77–9
Altman, Joel 144, 172 n.7
ambiguity 86–7, 92–8, 152
　of modal verbs 21–2, 29–30, 42, 92–8
　nuance 32, 35–6, 145
ambivalence 144–5
Amiens (*As You Like It*) 143
analogy 126
anaphora 157–8
and 153, 173 n.13
anger 51
antanaclasis 88
arguments 71–4
articles 129
articulacy 57, 83–4

As You Like It 24, 67, 133–61
　Amiens 143
　Celia 67, 154–5, 156–7
　conditionality 155–6
　drama 158–61
　Duke Senior 143
　education 138–50
　Ganymede (Rosalind) 147–8, 149, 159–60
　gender 156–7
　hypothesis 153–4
　if, use of 151–61
　Jaques 133, 134, 143–4
　Oliver 133–4
　Orlando 133–4, 157–8
　Phoebe 150
　Rosalind 67, 146–51, 155–6, 157, 159–61
　Silvius 158
　Touchstone 144–6, 151–2, 156–7
audience 20, 159
authority 22, 37–40, 49–52, 56, 59, 66, 109
　command 117–18
　domination 38–40, 46
　and loquacity 78–9
　royal 112–13, 128–9
　of women 77–82

Bakhtin, Mikhail 16
Bede, *Ecclesiastical History of the English People* 36–7
Benveniste, Emile 103
Bernardo (*Hamlet*) 66, 67
Bible, the 2–4, 164 n.7
bodies 23–4, 42, 106, 126, 128–9, 170 n.14
    and ritual 117, 119–20
Bolingbroke (*Richard II*) 110, 111–12
Brown, Penelope 120, 165 n.2

'Caedmon's Hymn' 36–7
Caesar, Philip 2–3
Caius Martius Coriolanus 25–7, 41–3, 45–61
Calvo, Clara 67
can 45
capacity 45
caricature 145–6
Celia (*As You Like It*) 67, 154–5, 156–7
challenge 155
characterization 9, 75–9, 82–3
characters 20, 66
Cheke, Sir John 4, 6
Chomsky, Noam 13, 15
class, social 1, 57, 138, 172 n.6. *See also* rank
classical language 4–6
classical literature 148–50
close reading 68–9, 70
coercion 46
collaborative discourse 96–8
command 117–18
'common' (definition) 1–2, 3–4, 162 n.4
common language 2–6, 25–8
communication

competence 13, 15, 58, 74, 83–4
    indirect 155–6
    miscommunication 91–3
    misunderstanding 92
    social 42–3
    and subtext 35–6
community 5, 28, 42, 117
competence, linguistic/communicative 13, 15, 58, 74, 83–4
competition 72–3
comprehension, lack of 93
concordances 8, 153–4, 174 n.16
conditionality 31, 39, 40, 152–3, 155–6, 159–60. *See also* possibility
conflict 29, 45–54, 71–4
    defiance 90, 94, 127–8, 155–6, 167 n.17
    disagreement 79–81, 155–6, 166 n.10
conjunctions 8, 9
    and 153, 173 n.13
    if 151–61, 173 n.12, 173 n.13, 174 n.15, 174 n.16
context 102–8
    historical 69
    and meaning 100–2, 103–4
    physical 104, 106, 119–20
    social 33, 35, 104–5, 108–9, 110–11, 117
    spatial 104, 105, 168–9 n.7
contradiction 81–2, 155–6
control
    of dialogue 48
    of discourse 22, 52–3, 54, 56–7, 117–18, 122
    domination 38–40, 46
    of future time 116
    of speech 45–6, 49–50, 54, 72–3

conversation 64, 166 n.6
  competitive 72–3
  conventions 67, 72
  and deictic markers 105–6
  interruption 56, 67, 80–1, 82, 91, 118
  turn-taking 67, 78, 79, 129
Coriolanus 21–2, 25–61
  and communication 42–3
  and community 25–8
  conflict, interpersonal 45–54
  and dialogue 43–7
  First Citizen 25–8
  futility of language 27–8
  and power 37–42
  and regulation of discourse 48–54
  and selfhood 28–9
  Sicinius 49–52, 56–7
  Volumnia 38–40, 45–7, 58–60
Coriolanus (Caius Martius) 25–7, 41–3, 45–61
courtly love 75–6, 149
Coverdale, Miles 2
Cox, Leonard 5
Craig, Hugh 14, 29, 162 n.6
Cressida (*Troilus and Cressida*) 74–81, 82–4, 89–98, 167 n.14, 167 n.16, 167 n.17
Cummings, Brian 11–12, 30, 40, 131, 137, 164 n.7

debate 144–5
defiance 90, 94, 127–8, 155–6, 167 n.17
deixis 23, 100, 102–8, 130–1, 168 n.7, 170 n.17
desire 29, 46, 75, 122–3
  shall as indicator of 36
  will as indicator of 44, 88, 93, 96
  wishes 89, 154

dialogue, dramatic 16–20, 32–3
  and deictic markers 105–6
  and discourse analysis 64–8
  interrogation 47–8
  interruption 56, 67, 80–1, 82, 91, 118
  and modal verbs 43–7
dialogue, 'real' 17–19, 64
Diomedes (*Troilus and Cressida*) 95–6
disagreement 79–81, 155–6, 166 n.10
discipline 139–40
disconnectedness 94–5
discourse
  collaborative 96–8
  control of 22, 52–3, 54, 56–7, 117–18, 120–1
  conversation 64, 166 n.6
    competitive 72–3
    conventions 67, 72
    and deictic markers 105–6
    turn-taking 67, 78, 79, 129
  dialogue, dramatic 16–20, 32–3
    and deictic markers 105–6
    and discourse analysis 64–8
    interrogation 47–8
    and modal verbs 43–7
  formality 100, 109, 117
  interrogation 47–8, 78, 91–3
  interruption 56, 67, 80–1, 82, 91, 118
  oration 26, 52–3
  performance 13, 16, 18, 19–20, 140
  public 117
  quarrels 71–4, 95–6
  'real' 17–19, 64

regulation of 48–9
repetition 7–8, 78, 85–6, 88, 111–12, 126
rhetoric 145–6
  anaphora 157–8
  antanaclasis 88
  of courtly love 75–6
  quaestio 144–5
  social exchange 15–16, 18–19
  as text 96–8
  wordplay 71–4, 88, 95–6, 110, 142
discourse analysis 16–18, 23, 64–70, 84–6, 165 n.2, 166 n.11
disruption 118–19
distance 104–5, 125–6, 129, 163 n.4, 167 n.16
domination 38–40, 48
drama 18, 158–61, 168 n.7
  dialogue, dramatic 16–20, 32–3
  and deictic markers 105–6
  and discourse analysis 64–8
  interrogation 47–8
  and modal verbs 43–7
  performance 13, 16, 18, 19–20, 140
Dubrow, Heather 105
Duke Senior (*As You Like It*) 143
duty 29, 33–4, 36–7, 43–4, 58, 122–3

early modern English 10–12, 30–2, 136–8, 173 n.12
education 133–50
  grammar schools 134–5, 136, 138–44, 172 n.6
Elam, Keir 18, 104, 106, 122, 130–1, 159, 168 n.3, 168 n.7
emphasis 94
English language

  development 4–5, 6, 11–12, 21–2, 30–1
  early modern 10–12, 30–2, 136–8, 173 n.12
  etymology 6, 31–2, 36, 37, 51–2, 83
  Old English 36–7
  See also grammar; rhetoric
Enterline, Lynn 139–40
eroticism 139–40
etymology 6, 31–2, 36, 37, 51–2, 83

'face' 66, 165 n.3
Falstaff 7–8
familiarity 109
fear 51–2
female characters
  authority of 77–82
  Celia (*As You Like It*) 67, 154–5, 156–7
  Cressida (*Troilus and Cressida*) 74–81, 82–4, 89–98, 167 n.14, 167 n.16, 167 n.17
  education 147
  Rosalind (*As You Like It*) 67, 146–51, 155–6, 157, 159–61
  silencing of 74, 75, 93
  speech of 82–3
  Volumnia (*Coriolanus*) 38–40, 45–7, 58–60
  See also gender
First Citizen (*Coriolanus*) 25–7
first person 112, 121–2, 123, 127–8
Fitzmaurice, Susan 29, 89, 104, 106, 111, 164 n.6
formalism 14
formality 100, 109, 117
frequency of word use 153–4, 174 n.16
functional grammar 84–6

futility, of language 27–8
future time 34, 38, 89, 116, 122–3
   intention 9, 41–2, 93–4, 96, 128
   possibility 29–30, 45, 152, 153, 159
   See also desire; volition

Ganymede (Rosalind, *As You Like It*) 147–8, 149, 159–60
gender 74, 82–3, 147–8, 156–7
grammar 15–16, 24, 135–6
   adverbs 126, 152
   articles 129
   changes 30–1
   early modern 11–12, 136–8
   functional 84–6
   imperatives 40, 48, 69, 91 (*see also must*)
   interrogatives 78
   inversion 124
   Lily, William, *Shorte Introduction of Grammar* 30, 134–5, 138–9, 148–9, 171–2 n.5
   and meaning 15–16
   in Middle Ages 137
   nouns 1, 86–7
   and politeness 151–2
   possessive adjectives 129
   prepositions 8
   sentences 15
   tenses 150–1
   verbs
      to be 150–1, 153
      had 152–3
      is 150–1
      lexical 30–1, 93
      modal (*see* modal verbs)
   See also pronouns

grammar schools 134–5, 136, 138–44, 172 n.6
Grice, H.P. 67

had 152–3
Halliday, M.A.K. 84–6, 96–8
Hamlet 2, 30–1, 64–7
Hanks, William F. 54–5, 103–8, 119, 128, 170 n.15, 170 n.19
hearing/listening 20, 159
Henry IV, Part 1 7–8
Henry VI, Part 1 142
Henry VI, Part 2 153
here 126
Herman, Vimala 15, 17–19, 46, 78, 105, 114, 118, 162 n.7
Holofernes (*Love's Labour's Lost*) 140
honorifics 23, 108–9, 111–12, 122–3
hope 89
Hope, Jonathan 11, 14, 133, 137, 154, 162 n.5
humanism 137
humour 140–2, 151–2
   caricature 145–6
   satire 142, 143–4
   wit 79, 83
   wordplay 2, 71–4, 88, 95–6, 110, 141
Hymes, Dell 15
hyperbole 75–6
hypothesis 153–4

I 121–2, 123, 127–8
identity 32, 54, 70–1, 74–5, 110–11, 128–9
   deictic markers of 103, 105
   indeterminate 121–4, 127

royal 112–15, 121–4, 126–7
See also selfhood; subjectivity
if 24, 151–61, 173 n.12, 173 n.13, 174 n.15, 174 n.16
imitation 140
imperatives 40, 48, 69, 91. *See also must*
impersonation 140
individuals 28, 42, 58, 71–2, 100, 110–11, 117
intention 9, 38, 41–2, 93–4, 96, 128
interpretation 29, 65, 86, 92–3, 101
interrogation 47–8, 78, 91–3
interrogatives 78
interruption 56, 67, 80–1, 82, 91, 118
intimacy 104–5
is 150–1

Jakobson, Roman 13–14
Jaques (*As You Like It*) 133, 134, 143–4
John of Gaunt (*Richard II*) 107–8, 110
Julius Caesar 34–5

king 108, 111–12, 122–3
King John 35
Kuhn, Maura Slattery 153–4

language
  classical 4–6
  common 2–6, 25–8
  etymology 6, 31–2, 36, 37, 51–2, 83–4
  futility of 27–8
  poetic 34–5, 157–9
  usage 32–3, 108, 136
  vernacular 4–6
  'vulgar' 3–4

See also discourse; English language; grammar; Latin; linguistics; rhetoric
Latin 4–6, 137, 138–9, 140–1, 142, 146, 148–50
Levinson, Steven C. 104, 108, 114–15, 120, 125, 165 n.3
Lévi-Strauss, Claude 13
lexical cohesion 85–6, 88–9
lexical verbs 30–1, 93
Lily, William, *Shorte Introduction of Grammar* 30, 134–5, 138–9, 148–9, 171–2 n.5
linguistics 10–11, 13–15
  deixis 23, 100, 102–8, 130–1, 168–9 n.7, 170 n.17
  discourse analysis 16–18, 23, 64–70, 84–6, 165 n.2, 166 n.11
  historical 32–3
  origo 105, 123, 168 n.6
  pragmatics 23, 85, 100–2, 155
  semantics 100–1
  sociolinguistics 32–3
listening/hearing 20, 159
loquacity 43, 78
Love's Labour's Lost 2, 140

Magnusson, Lynne 14, 64, 68, 165 n.2, 167 n.18
male characters 74, 147. *See also* Bolingbroke; Coriolanus; gender; Jaques; John of Gaunt; Orlando; Pandarus; Richard II; Touchstone; Troilus
Marlowe, Christopher 35, 150
may 29–30
meaning

ambiguous 29–30, 86–7, 92–8, 152–3
  construction of 73–4
  and context 100–2, 103–4
  encoded 35–6
  and grammar 15–16
  individualized 71–2
  nuanced 32, 35–6, 145
  polysemous 1–2, 45, 86–7
  pragmatic 101–2
  reception of 20
  relational 15–16
metaphor 42, 126
mimesis 18–19
miscommunication 91–3
misunderstanding 92
mockery 71–4
modal verbs 9, 11, 21–3, 28–32, 33–4
  can 45
  may 29–30
  must 29, 36–7, 39, 40, 46
  ought 29, 30, 36–7
  shall 21–2, 31–2, 36–42, 164 n.7
    indicating desire 36
    and power 49–53, 55–7, 116, 122–3
  shall versus *will* 31–2, 44–5, 58
  will 22–3, 87–96
    indicating desire 44, 88, 93, 96
    indicating volition 30, 33–4, 39, 40, 92–3, 123
    and power 127–8
  would 31, 39, 40
monosyllables 7–8, 90, 102, 123
Much Ado About Nothing 141
Mulcaster, Richard 4–5
must 29, 36–7, 39, 40, 45, 128
my 129

names 108–11, 166 n.4
Nash, Walter 64–7
nouns 1, 86–7
nuance 32, 35–6, 145

obligation 29, 33–4, 36–7, 58, 122–3
Old English 36–7
Oliver (*As You Like It*) 133–4
oration 26, 52–3
origo (reference point) 105, 123, 168 n.6
Orlando (*As You Like It*) 133–4, 157–8
ought 29, 30, 36–7
Ovid 148

Pandarus (*Troilus and Cressida*) 71–4, 79–82
paraphrase 65
Parker, Patricia 12, 84
pedantry 146
performance 13, 16, 18, 19–20, 140
permission 29, 45, 51
Phoebe (*As You Like It*) 150
poetic language 34–5, 157–9
politeness 120–1, 151–2, 165 n.3
possessive adjectives 129
possibility 29–30, 45, 152, 153, 159. *See also* conditionality
poststructuralism 13, 14
power 29, 30, 32, 36, 128
  command 117–18
  domination 37–40, 46
  imbalance 115
  lack of 41–2, 54–5, 115
  and *shall*, use of 49–53, 55–7, 116, 122–3
  social 39–40, 115–16
  See also authority; control

pragmatics 23, 85, 100–2, 155
prediction 34
prepositions 8
Prince Hal (*Henry IV Part 1*) 7–8
prolixity 43, 78
promise 34
pronouns 8, 9
    demonstrative 125–7, 129
    personal 23, 53–4, 103, 104
    I 121–2, 123, 127–8
    royal 112–14, 121–2
    we 112, 123
props 129
Protestantism 2–4
proximity 125–6, 129
puns 2, 87, 88, 110, 141

quaestio 144–5
quarrels 71–4, 95–6
questions 77–9, 91–3, 144–5

rank 39–40, 50, 51, 53, 78. *See also* social class
Rape of Lucrece, The 75–7
readers 159
realism 18–19
real/unreal boundary 156–7
reception 20, 92, 159
redirection 118–19
regulation 48–54, 136
relationships
    boundaries of 39–40
    construction of 15–16, 32, 167 n.18
    social 9, 107, 110–11
religion 2–4, 164 n.7
repetition 7–8, 78, 85–6, 88, 111–12, 126
rhetoric 145–6
    anaphora 157–8
    antanaclasis 88
    of courtly love 75–6
    quaestio 144–5
Richard II (character) 112–14, 121–8
Richard II (play) 23–4, 99–131
    Bolingbroke 110, 111–12
    deposition scene (4.1) 124–30
    John of Gaunt 107–8, 110
    names 108–11
    ritual 117–21, 127–8
    and royal identity 112–15, 121–4
riddles 155
ritual 117–21, 127–8, 169 n.11, 170 n.15, 170 n.19
Rosalind (*As You Like It*) 67, 146–51, 155–6, 157, 159–61
royalty 112–15, 121–4, 128–9
rules 48–54, 136

Sander, Nicholas 3–4
satire 142, 143–4
Saussure, Ferdinand de 13–14, 103
schoolmasters 145–8
schools, grammar 133–5, 136, 138–44, 172 n.6
selfhood 9, 52, 53–4, 103. *See also* identity; subjectivity
self-positioning 28–9, 47, 57–8
self-reference 109–10, 113, 114, 121–2, 123–4
semantics 100–1
semiotics 13, 18
sentences 15, 124
separation 94–5
sex/sexuality 83–4, 139–40
shall 21–2, 36–42, 164 n.7
    and power 49–53, 55–7, 116, 122–3
    versus *will* 31–2, 44–5, 46, 58

Sicinius (*Coriolanus*) 49–52, 56–7
Sidney, Philip 35
silence/silencing 74, 75, 93
Silvius (*As You Like It*) 158
small words 7–9
social class 1, 57, 138, 172 n.6. *See also* rank
social exchange 15–16, 18–19
sociolinguistics 32–3
Sonnets 142, 153
speakers 19, 26
   agency 35
   attitudes of 152, 155
   as collaborators 96–8
   and deictic markers 105–6
   position of 28–9, 122, 123, 128, 130
   power of 37
   self-perception 35
speech
   control of 45–6, 49–50, 54, 72–3
   and deictic markers 105–6
   permitted 26–7
   silencing of 74, 75
   of women 82–3
status 39–40, 50, 51, 53, 78. *See also* social class
structuralism 13–14
subjectivity 106–7, 130–1, 166 n.4. *See also* identity; selfhood
subtext 35–6, 155–6
syllables 7–8, 45–6, 90, 102, 123

talkativeness 43, 78
Taming of the Shrew, The 142
Tannen, Deborah 17
teachers 145–8
Tempest, The 142, 153
tenses 150–1
Terence 149

text 35–6, 96–8, 155–6
that 126, 129
the 129
there 129
third person 121–2, 123
this 126, 129
threat 34, 113–14
titles 23, 108–9, 111–12, 122–3
Titus Andronicus 141–2
to be 150–1, 153
Touchstone (*As You Like It*) 144–6, 151–2, 156–7
tragic hero 42–3
translation 2–4, 36–7, 143, 146
Troilus (character) 71–4, 90–3, 97–8
Troilus and Cressida 22–3, 63–98, 165 n.1
   Alexander 77–9
   ambiguity 86–7, 92–8
   characterization 75–9
   Cressida 74–81, 89–98, 167 n.14, 167 n.16, 167 n.17
   Diomedes 95–6
   discourse analysis 84–6
   miscommunication 91–3
   Pandarus 71–4, 79–82
   questions 77–9
   wordplay 71–4, 87, 88
turn-taking, in conversation 67, 78, 79, 129
Twelfth Night 153

understanding, lack of 92
usage 32–3, 108, 136
utterances 15, 34, 65, 79, 81, 170 n.16

vehemence 94
verbs
   to be 150–1, 153

had 152–3
  lexical 30–1, 93
  modal (*see* modal verbs)
vernacular language 4–6
voices 26, 163 n.2
  multiple 25–6, 57
volition 9, 29–30, 75, 84, 128, 154
  and power 46–7, 58–60, 127–8
  will as indicator of 30, 33–4, 39, 40, 92–3, 123
Volumnia (*Coriolanus*) 38–40, 45–7, 58–60
'vulgar' language 3–4

Wallis, Bishop John 34
was 150–1
we 112, 123
were 153
wh-interrogatives 78
will 22–3, 87–96
  indicating desire 44, 88, 93, 96
  indicating volition 30, 33–4, 39, 40, 92–3, 123
  and power 127–8
  versus *shall* 31–2, 44–5, 58
wishes 89, 154
wit 79, 83
Witmore, Michael 154, 162 n.5
word frequency 153–4, 174 n.16
word order 124
wordplay 71–4, 88, 95–6, 110, 142
would 31, 39, 40

www.ingramcontent.com/pod-product-compliance
Lightning Source LLC
Chambersburg PA
CBHW052044300426
44117CB00012B/1971